DEDICATION

For my beloved bride and our remarkable children, with all my love, and for the God who saved a wretch like me, with profound gratitude.

Comfort
in the Shadow:
A Spiritual Memoir

Bob L.

CONTENTS

FORWARD

This book is what I wish I could teach my children about God, life, work, love, parenting, grief and dying. What my kids do with these observations is entirely their business.

Thirty years ago, Alcoholics Anonymous saved my life and reset it on a productive course. I couldn't tell my story without mentioning AA's part in it. Out of respect for AA's traditions, I am not adding my full name to this text.

NON COINCIDENCES

I was raised to believe in science. I still do. Medical science has slowed incurable cancer long enough for me to write this.

I was trained to be a professional skeptic, cross-examining self-proclaimed experts to prove they did not follow the scientific method. I'm still a skeptic. It's handy for parsing fake news and investment offers.

For a long time, my scientific skepticism kept me from believing in God. I thought that if man couldn't understand God or explain how God could do what God does, then God couldn't be. People in a simpler time must have invented God to comprehend what science would ultimately reveal to be the blind work of physics, biology, chemistry, and statistical probability. There could be no greater intelligence than ours.

A foxhole prayer thirty years ago triggered a white light experience that challenged my agnosticism. A friend then suggested that I reexamine some of the events I had reflexively dismissed as coincidences. Reconsidered with an open mind, it was evident that a few of the synchronicities happening around me could not happen by accident. The

1

odds were too long for so many independent variables to randomly align so elegantly. I was an actor with free will, it seemed, but there was an author-director offstage who occasionally weighed in.

This book recounts some of the episodes from my life that convinced me something is afoot in the world beyond natural law and chance, and that the mysterious force that orchestrates so much of our lives is loving, omniscient, and powerful. It was freeing for me to learn that God does not have to be understood, just experienced. A reader as skeptical as I was may not be convinced by any account of secondhand miracles, but perhaps this book will help her perceive her own miracles. As C.S. Lewis put it: "We may ignore, but we can nowhere evade the presence of God. The world is crowded with Him. He walks everywhere incognito."

For those who can accept the existence of divine mystery, I pass along some of the practical advice others shared with me on how to mature my belief and apply it in my life. Faith is a great comfort.

In writing this, I share the hope Rev. Nadia Bolz-Weber describes at the end of her book of personal spiritual vignettes, *Accidental Saints*:

> I want [readers] to see how real grace and mercy and forgiveness and brokenness and beauty are around them, in their lives. I guarantee the things that happen to me are happening to them, too … [T]he glory of God in the midst of our crap is revealed all the time, all around us. What I hope is that people would read the book and see that and realize how transformative it can be.

A WHITE LIGHT EXPERIENCE

My willingness to consider the possibility that God exists began with a revelation.

I was thirty-three and hopelessly off the rails. No matter what I wanted to do or said I would do, every day I started to drink again, after work during the week and in the morning on weekends, and I continued to drink until I passed out. My second wife was leaving, following my first wife's exit three years earlier. Important people at work were noticing how much I drank. Soon I wouldn't be able to hide my second wife's departure from them and they would know something was seriously wrong with me. I was estranged from my family. I felt too dirty to be around them. I was afraid to go out. The booze and drugs dictated my behavior and I didn't know what I might say or do. I was snorting cocaine whenever I could, but it no longer brought the lift I craved, just the crash. I hated every one of the thirty or more cigarettes I smoked from waking till passing out, but I could not quit them. My life had escaped me. I was enslaved and dying in a foreign place, far from everything I had hoped for.

I decided to sell my apartment in Westchester County and move to a ramshackle cottage supported by stilts on the steep western bank of the Hudson River, just south of the Tappan Zee Bridge. It would be a horrible commute from that cottage to my job in Manhattan, but I thought that if my second wife and I could see the sun set over the river every night the way it set over the hill across the lake from my family's cottage in the Finger Lakes, we could calm down, stop drinking and drugging so much, and get our lives back together. Our real problem was that we were country mice and needed long vistas.

Years later, I realized that among the many flaws in this plan, unlike our family cottage on the eastern shore of the lake facing west, the cottage I was buying stood on the western bank of the river facing east. The sun sets behind the cottage, not over the river in front like it did in my fantasies. This would undoubtedly have created a disappointing first evening on the porch if I had completed the purchase.

In my haste to revive my second wife's and my dead relationship before the corpse went cold, I did not have time to consider details like where the sun actually sets. I signed a contract and made a down payment on the cottage the day I looked at it and immediately prepared to put my co-op on the market. A co-op bubble had popped the year before and the market was flooded with unsold apartments. I would have to fix mine up to get the price I needed to make the cottage plan work.

The first step was getting the apartment painted. I left a message for the realtor who sold me my co-op asking her for a referral to a painter. She called back when I was out and left a return message with three phone numbers. The second on the list, Chuck, answered when I called.

The next week, Chuck and his partner Ruari began painting my apartment. I was certain that Ruari, being Irish, must be stealing my booze but I couldn't prove it. I made plans to mark the fluid level on the label of the bottle I was drinking from so I could confront Ruari with his pilferage, but I always ended up too drunk to remember to set the trap. While I could never prove that he was stealing from me, I remained convinced. I glowered at Ruari over our secret sometimes so he would know that I was on to him.

A counselor told my second wife to go to an AA meeting and I said I would go with her. She returned from our upstate hometown where she was living with her new boyfriend for a few days but left again for good before the meeting we planned to attend.

The morning she left, I had a moment of clarity and saw how lost I was. My second wife was giving her exit speech in the open doorway of my apartment with the morning sun backlighting her when it struck me that what she was saying to me was eerily similar to what my first wife had said when she called me from Paris after she left. It hit me that these two very different women were leaving me three years apart and the only thing they had in common was me. I was the problem, not them, and I couldn't pretend otherwise any longer. Soon everyone would know what a wreck my life had become.

As my second wife closed the door behind her, a dam broke in me. I cried and cried on my couch. I tried to compose myself and walked down the hill to the train station to head to work. I was still in tears when I got to my station, so I set out for the next station two miles away, hoping the walk would settle my emotions. A mile in, on that crisp November morning, something shifted. For the first time in memory, I felt hope that something might now change to end the long years of darkness.

I hardly drank the rest of the workweek. Midweek, I called my friend Jack, who had joined AA three years earlier. I told him that my wife's drinking was out of control and now she was gone. I asked Jack what I should do about my wife's drinking, but he would only talk about me.

5

"Do you think you have a problem with alcohol?" Jack asked.

I thought hard. I knew that if you admit to a drinking problem, people will tell you to quit or moderate. I also knew, after countless failed attempts, that I could not possibly do that. But that day, for some reason, knowing that Jack had been where I was and in his three years of sobriety he had never challenged my drinking, I felt safe enough to answer his question without deflecting it.

"Jack," I said after a long pause, "I drink more than I want to."

"Well," Jack said. "You can go to Al-Anon [a wonderful support group for families of alcoholics] and cry about your wife's drinking, or you can go to AA and laugh about yours."

As a result of talking with Jack, and even though I could no longer pretend to be going to support my absent wife, I attended my first AA meeting that Sunday night. Halfway through, I decided I didn't like it and would bolt the instant it ended. When it was finally over, people started chatting with each other and I quietly slid my chair back to leave.

As I braced to stand, a hand appeared on my shoulder. It belonged to Chuck, the apartment painter. His helper and presumptive booze-stealer Ruari was next to him. Later, I saw the realtor who referred them to me at another meeting. It was a cabal. Chuck asked me if I would like to join Ruari and him by the coffee pot, where there were cookies.

We smoked and ate cookies and talked. I wanted to talk about my wife's drinking, but like Jack before him, Chuck kept returning to my own.

"Have you ever had trouble with the law over drinking?" he asked.

"No." I had been ticketed for things I did while drunk but had never been expressly charged for drinking, except as a juvenile, and that conviction was expunged from my record after I completed probation.

"Have you had trouble at work from your drinking?"

"Nope." I had been fired for tardiness, poor performance, and absenteeism caused by drinking, but never for drinking on the job.

"Are you drinking in the morning?"

"Nope." I only drank in the morning on days when I wasn't working, or on an early flight home. That obviously didn't count. Everyone does that. Why else would they have champagne brunches or Bloody Mary mix on airplane breakfast carts?

On Chuck went, slowly convincing me that whatever I was, I wasn't an alcoholic. Chuck and Ruari had noticed with amusement how my booze evaporated overnight and saw its impact on me in the morning when they arrived for work. Chuck assumed that I hadn't wandered into an AA meeting by accident and kept pressing on. I was getting tired of it.

"I'll bet you really tied one on this week, didn't you?" He smirked like we were in on some big secret.

"No, I didn't. I only drank near beer all week, had two beers at a co-worker's going away party on Friday, then I came home." Take that, Chuck. I omitted the fact that I left the party after two beers because I was about to start crying again.

"What about last night?" Chuck asked, smiling like he knew the answer and just wanted me to say it. "Did you hit it hard then?"

Enough. It was time to shut this down.

"I wanted to drink last night, but all I had in the house was a half bottle of scotch and I poured it down the sink." That was that. What alcoholic could pour the only booze in the house down the sink?

Chuck paused and looked me in the eyes through his thick glasses, spattered with specks of Atrium White paint.

He wasn't smirking anymore. "Bob," he said carefully, "do you think that social drinkers have to pour their scotch down the sink to stay away from it?"

There was no arguing with him. Only an alcoholic must put a physical barrier between himself and the booze to accomplish what his will cannot. That was it. There are only two kinds of drinkers, social drinkers and alcoholics, and I was not a social drinker: I was an alcoholic. Alcoholism was a disease, they had said at the meeting, and I had it. These people had a cure for alcoholism. I was in. Years of denial evaporated just like that.

At an AA meeting Chuck took me to the following week, I timidly announced to the group that I thought I was an alcoholic. Breaking the omertà was the last thing my disease wanted. Our secret kept me separate from everyone. My disease jumped all over me on the drive home. "You're not an alcoholic!" it insisted in the voice I thought of as the sound of my own thinking. "You're just saying that to try to fit in because you're lonely and they're nice. You don't belong in AA. You don't have a right to be there. You're just a guy who got a little out of hand. You can control your drinking. You have a job and wear a suit and own a co-op. You're not on the street."

By the time I reached my apartment, I had a strong urge to drink. I screwed up the courage to call Chuck and, after beating around the bush for ten minutes, finally confessed that I was thinking about drinking. Chuck offered three suggestions, two of them rational. He said I should eat some chocolate. That made sense. Chocolate releases serotonin, a neurotransmitter that makes you happy. He said I should take a hot bath. That made sense too. Hot baths release endorphins, another feel-good chemical. With his third suggestion, Chuck stopped making sense. Chuck suggested that I get on my knees and ask God to keep me from drinking.

I got off the phone as quickly as I could now that Chuck had shown his spots as a religious nut and acted on his two rational suggestions. I ate some chocolate, and it helped. I took a hot bath and it helped more. Then, the craving came back.

I knew that I could not resist that craving. Like a zombie, I would soon be out of the house, sleepwalking to the neighborhood deli. I would be three beers into the six-pack I would buy at the deli before it hit me that I was drinking again after swearing that I would stop. It would be too late. The booze would be running the show and there was no telling where it would take me or when I would stop drinking again. I had found myself drinking when I said I wouldn't hundreds of times.

I was out of ideas. Repellent as it seemed, all I had left to combat the craving was Chuck's third suggestion. The problem with Chuck's suggestion that I ask God for help was that I did not believe in God. I would have liked the comfort believers claimed, but I could not find a way to accept the idea of a supernatural entity. It seemed like something for simple people, not for educated, intelligent professionals like me.

Shoulders slumped in utter defeat, glowing with embarrassment that I had been driven to such a pollyannaish step, remembering all the people I had silently and openly ridiculed for praying to a God that did not exist, I slipped to my knees beneath my sixth floor window so anyone who had climbed the church steeple across the street to spy on me would not see what a fool I was about to make of myself. I lowered my head to the floor and said to the rug: "Please help me."

I could not have anticipated what happened next. Immediately, a wave of peace washed over me. For the first time in memory, I felt that everything was going to be OK. My body relaxed. Time softened, and the light suffused the room with a gentle glow. The craving to drink was gone and never returned.

I eased onto my futon and lay face down. I felt like someone was slowly stroking my back, but it didn't freak me out. I felt safe, loved, and hopeful. The constant looping of my worries was stilled. I drifted into sleep and slept deeply through the night, more deeply than I had since childhood, more deeply than I have in the thirty years since.

BELIEVING IS SEEING

The morning after my "white light" encounter with God, the skeptical part of my wiring reactivated. Old ways of seeing the world die hard. There can't be a God, my brain shouted. Maybe it was a hallucination. Maybe I was detoxing. Maybe it was wishful thinking, grasped at so I could fit in with Chuck and the AA crowd the way I tried to believe in the burning bush and Jonah and the whale to fit in with my Sunday school classmates.

But there was something so different about my experience, so otherworldly, that I could not dismiss it as imagined. Whatever words I use to describe it fail. To communicate, there must be a shared understanding of the phenomena the words describe, or at least a shared metaphor to relate it to: it was like this, or like that. This was not like anything in the material realm. It's why we revert to iconography – halos and wings – to depict something so ineffable it defies any attempt to accurately convey it. It was a physical encounter, durable and different in kind from the fragile skeins of delusion, experienced outside the normal five senses in some deeper part of my being – my soul, perhaps? – separate from my mind. Even against the challenge of my abiding cynicism this felt real.

Contrary to everything I thought that I would ever be able to believe, I now knew something was going on in the world that I did not expect and could not explain. I had been wrong about the fundamental nature of existence. There was a mystical, unseen element operating outside reason and outside anything science would ever be able to dissect. The world was enchanted.

Struggling to adjust to this tectonic shift in my conception of reality, I heard someone say at an AA meeting that I could "consider the possibility that there are no coincidences, that everything happens for a reason." That concept was the key for my new faith and my longstanding scientific skepticism to coexist. Somehow, once I was able to consider the possibility that there was a higher power, I could see things happening that could only be reasonably explained as the actions of a loving, omnipotent God. I couldn't see God, but I could see clear evidence of God's divine intervention. It's like seeing trees dance outside the window and knowing there must be wind to animate them, even if I can't see or hear or feel it. Saint Augustine said the reward of faith in the unseen is to begin to see what we believe. When I allowed that ancient grace could still exist in our cold, empirical world, I could see its unmistakable works.

I still believe in natural science and I still believe in probabilities. But when things happen that could not happen within natural laws and credible probabilities, I believe that something supernatural, beyond nature or chance, has intervened. The rest of the book describes some of the non-coincidences which convinced me that God exists, that God has a purpose for us, that God loves us, and that God can and does intervene in human lives for good.

THE RICHMOND ANGEL

I first recognized God's handiwork in my life one Sunday evening a few days after my white light experience. The night before, I attended two back-to-back Saturday night AA meetings. I was still obsessing over whether to try to woo my second wife her back. Now that I was sober, maybe she would clean up too and it would all work out. But did we really have anything in common besides drinking? Beneath my terror of being alone, wasn't there also relief that the pretense that we that belonged together had finally collapsed?

I hardly heard anything at the first meeting. Unused to living without sedation, my mind oscillated uncontrollably between the mess of my drinking past and all the trouble I envisioned ahead of me.

Having heard so little at the first meeting beyond my own fretful thoughts, I was still anxious when it ended. I stayed for the second, more intimate meeting, hoping it would calm me. The meeting leaders turned down the lights in the big church hall and gathered a small group of us in a candlelit semicircle around that night's speaker. I was less self-conscious in the dark and settled down enough to hear some of what the speaker at the second meeting said.

He suggested, among other things, that we could decline the key to a hotel minibar when we traveled. I was on the road a hundred days a year and could see the evident good sense in refusing the minibar key; I just never realized I had a right to do that. It's a good tip, but it's not often offered in AA meetings. In three decades of regular attendance, I've heard the minibar advice no more than three times, which works out to roughly once every fifteen hundred meetings.

It is remarkable that eighteen hours after hearing that rarely-dispensed advice I found myself checking into a hotel in Richmond with a desk clerk handing me a minibar key. Remembering the suggestion from the night before, I declined it. I feared the desk clerk would see me as unmanly, but he was nonchalant. He didn't even sneer.

Declining the minibar key felt like a small victory. There was a jolt of electricity when I recognized that I had been given the information to address this situation just hours before I needed it. In the time since, I've come to see that's often how God works.

I was nervous about my first sober business trip. It was a trial, which is variously thrilling and terrifying but always exhausting, and it would last a couple of weeks. I wasn't senior enough for a speaking part in a major trial, but I had fairly urgent backroom duties. I would need to meet the real time pressures of keeping documents and witnesses teed up, and I would need to quickly research and brief novel issues as they arose, often deep into the night. Two weeks of that would be draining.

We were defending a motorcycle company. I was assigned to that account because I rode motorcycles. I had many boozy misadventures with the hard-drinking, shrapnel-scarred, Purple Heart Vietnam infantry vet who was the company's engineering witness. Another corporate witness, a lawyer, was a full-blown alcoholic. I knew they would both pressure me to drink with them and I worried about straining the firm's relationship with our biggest client if I declined.

The desk clerk handed my room key to an elderly black man of perhaps fifty. I had driven to Richmond with a dozen boxes of trial documents. I felt pretentious using a bellman – country boys do for themselves – but it was a necessary extravagance. We loaded the boxes on a cart, which he wheeled to my room.

The bellman opened the door to my suite, unpacked the boxes, and explained the hotel's amenities. I was mortified when he pointed out, in addition to the locked minibar, a small refrigerator, unlocked and stocked with cold beer. It might as well have been a buzzing rattlesnake.

"Can you take that beer out of here?" I asked tightly, panic rising at this unforeseen threat.

"They might charge you for the beer," the bellman warned.

"I don't care!" I blurted out, the urgency in my voice surprising me. "I don't drink and I don't want to be around it!"

The bellman studied me for a moment, then smiled warmly. "I don't drink either," he said. He reached into his pants pocket, pulled out a big bronze coin, and handed it to me. It had the AA triangle in a circle logo on one side and a Roman numeral XIII on the other.

"I haven't had a drink in thirteen years," the bellman told me as I studied the coin. I told him that I hadn't drunk in two weeks and was going to AA. He pulled a pen from his vest pocket and a sheet of paper from the bedside notepad. He wrote down his name, his telephone number, and the address of a nearby AA clubhouse. "I'm here every day this week," he said. "If you need to talk to someone at night, you call me at this number anytime."

Every morning and every evening as I passed through the lobby, the bellman smiled and asked me how I was doing. It wasn't just a pleasantry; he cared. If none of my colleagues from the trial were around and if he wasn't busy with another guest, I reported how it was going.

I didn't make it to a meeting in Richmond, and my clients did try to pressure me into drinking with them. Knowing that the bellman was there, that he knew my secret, and that he hadn't drunk in thirteen years made me feel like I wasn't alone and I could get through it.

I was still suspicious of my newfound openness to the possibility of divine intervention, but it was impossible to mistake how elegantly things had come together. Something possessed me to stay for the second AA meeting the night before I left for Richmond. Notwithstanding my difficulty paying attention, I heard a bit of rarely offered information at that meeting hours before I would need it. That information empowered me to decline the minibar key.

Then, I had to use a bellman for perhaps my second time ever instead of toting my bags myself, as a man ought. We entered one of only a handful of hotel rooms among the hundreds I've encountered in decades of traveling that had beer in an unlocked refrigerator separate from the locked minibar. Seeing my minibar victory imperiled, I panicked, and before I could think about it, I implored the bellman to remove the beer. This was wildly uncharacteristic behavior for me.

Beyond all the things which had to line up to set the stage to this point, what are the odds that when I asked for help staying away from the beer I would turn out to have a bellman with thirteen years of sobriety in AA, who, seeing my panic about the booze, would then put his job at risk by breaking his anonymity with a guest? I submit that there are too many stacked improbabilities for all this to happen by chance. It wasn't an accident. Natural laws were trumped. Something supernatural was going on.

A couple weeks after the Richmond trial, I attended an AA meeting where the topic was AA's Third Step, which urges members to decide to "turn our life and our will over to the care of God, as we understand Him." I had glimpsed a higher power's movement in my life, but I certainly didn't understand God enough to turn my life and will over to Him.[1] Before I entrusted my life to God, I wanted to know how God could do what God did and why He acted so unpredictably, showing mercy here while allowing injustice there.

At the Third Step meeting, a gnarled World War II Marine who had crawled toward Japan through the hell of the Pacific island battles said in a gravelly voice that turning his life and will over to God was like walking to the end of a diving board and standing above a pool. He could get to the end of the diving board on logic and will, but eventually he had to jump, trusting that it would be alright. That leap could only be made on faith, not on certainty. Someone else added that at the end of the diving board there was a binary choice: God either was or God wasn't. If God was, then it would be pointless not to surrender to His omnipotence. I now knew that God was.

Driving home from the meeting, I sat at a stoplight, bedeviled by a whirlwind of obsessive worries. It struck me then that I could not bear the anxiety of living unsedated in a world without a loving higher power, where the only forces at play were physics, instincts, logic, biology, probabilities and my will; a world where the only hope for improving my odds against natural forces and Darwinian competition was to figure things out and then plan and then manipulate events better than whoever else was vying for the limited resources of money, power, romance, and the fleeting security they might bring in a hostile realm of scarcity.

Waiting out the red light, I realized that I could not live sober without God. I wasn't walking out on a diving board, I was walking the plank, with the cutlass of my anxiety prodding me forward. I couldn't go back. I had to jump. In the moment before the light turned green, I took AA's third step. I decided that I had to live the spiritual life they talked about, whatever that entailed. I had to follow God, whoever He was and wherever He took me. There was no other choice. I have spent the next three decades, with limited but increasing success, trying to put that decision into practice.

FOLLOWING THE NAZARENE

[M]ystical experience needs some form of dogma in order not to dissipate into moments of spiritual intensity that are merely personal ...

Christian Wiman – *My Bright Abyss: Meditation of a Modern Believer*

With the experience in the Richmond hotel added to the white light experience in my apartment, I began to have more confidence that there might be a higher power that could give my life direction. Initially, I could best conceptualize this higher power in Eastern mystical terms. There was a flow to the universe, the Tao, and to the extent I aligned myself with it, primarily through meditation, life would be easier than if I tried to swim against that impersonal current. The version of the *Tao Te Ching* I read was freely translated by Stephen Mitchell, who interpreted the text from an avowedly Zen Buddhist perspective, offering rich notes on each verse which piqued my interest in Zen.

AA encourages meditation practice but doesn't favor any meditative school or tradition. After reading a breezy overview of meditation techniques I picked up in an airport bookshop (*How to Meditate: A Guide to Self-Discovery* by Lawrence LeShan), I tried Zen breath counting meditation and liked it. My Zen practice was shaped by Shunryu Suzuki's classic introduction to Japanese Zen, *Zen Mind, Beginner's Mind*. Charlotte Joko Beck's *Everyday Zen* helped me envision Zen concepts through a contemporary American cultural lens. I began to sit zazen with a local Zen group twice a week in an old Quaker chapel and meditated at home most mornings.

Zen meditation practice is deceptively simple. Sit on a cushion and assume a solid position – in my case, a half lotus – with spine straight (imagine a string lifting the back of the head), chin down, eyes soft, face relaxed. Focus attention on the breathing, counting one breath in through the nose and down into the belly, one breath out. Try to release the tension you notice in your body. Try to let the breathing fall into a deep, natural rhythm like ocean waves. Count ten breaths in and out, then repeat, for twenty minutes.

The problem, of course, is my mind. It wants all my attention all the time. It constantly intrudes, interrupting my focus on the breath moving into and out of my body with skittering worries, minor physical discomforts, guesses at the future, replays of the past. If I realize I am no longer focusing on my breath, I was taught to just notice that I am thinking and return to my breathing, starting over at one. Many days I am too distracted to ever make it to ten. While the interruptions are frustrating, part of the process is learning not to chastise myself for being diverted. That only makes it harder to settle back into my breathing. Just notice the thoughts and return to the breath, over and over.

By noting the continual mental interruptions, I became more familiar with how my thought stream kept returning to my favorite fears and obsessions. After a while, I was able to say to myself: "Oh, it's just that again," and quickly return to my breathing. Learning to notice and unemotionally course-correct my attention drift without adding unproductive self-criticism helped me put away the scourge when I noticed myself behaving unskillfully outside the meditation setting. When I saw that I had gone off course, I could focus on resetting and repairing any damage I had caused without beating the tar out of myself. That started a virtuous cycle. When I ramped down the harsh judgment of my own failings, I was quicker to forgive others'. When I became less critical and more compassionate toward others, I was much kinder with myself, which made me happier and more useful to my higher power.

I had one brief experience of having a still mind – free of chatter, fully experiencing the moment with no intellectual distance, no mental cataloguing, no judgment. It was like slipping beneath a roiling ocean surface to the deep, quiet drift underneath. It happened on a weekend silent retreat, called a sesshin. My Zen group sat zazen, walked, ate, did our chores, and slept, all in silence, for two days. We spoke only for a few moments each afternoon in an individual meeting with our Zen priest, who checked in to see where we were getting stuck and to ensure that we didn't go off the rails in the silent struggle with our incessant egos.

Toward the end of the second afternoon, after many hours the previous day and a half wrestling with all the demons who can appear when I am alone with my mind, it happened. The noise in my head stopped. The pain in my legs became immaterial. I heard the others' tummies rumbling in the stillness. A leaf fell outside the window and its shadow moved across the barnwood floor of the retreat house. Motes of dust floated in a shaft of light before me. I was completely peaceful, completely absorbed. There was no separation between me and everything around me. It was sublime.

AA's Twelve Steps, derived from a Christian revivalist movement called the Oxford Group, envision God as more interactive than Eastern mysticism's impersonal flow. AA hastens to add that every member is free to conceive of their higher power as they might, and it expressly encourages non-Christians to adapt AA principles to other faith traditions.[2] Still, while workarounds are welcomed, AA's steps and literature are premised on the Pauline Christian precepts of an omnipotent God in eternal conflict with, but never vanquished by, a dark power that is stronger than the human will. When that dark force, "cunning, baffling, and powerful," in AA's words, overcomes us, only God's direct intervention can relieve us from its predations.[3]

AA's rooting in Christian dualism was most evident to me when I began trying to understand and employ the Sixth and Seventh Steps, urging us to become "entirely ready to have God remove all these defects of character" identified in our Fourth Step self-inventory, and then to "humbly ask Him to remove our shortcomings." With continuing sobriety, I recognized, as the AA literature suggested I would, that I had deeply ingrained negative behaviors besides drinking which I could not will away. When those behaviors bothered me enough that I was ready to be done with them at any cost, and when I had convinced myself through extended efforts that I could not control or eliminate them through strength of will, I resorted, as I had with alcohol, to prayer. When I was truly humbled, the same result followed. God intervened and the behavior was relieved, as long as I continued to be willing to cooperate with God.

Through this empirical process of trying to control my character defects only to find that God alone could relieve the most resilient ones, I came to see God as something other than an impersonal flow for me to align with. God seemed divinely interactive, at times directly responding to my heartfelt requests for His help in discerning and following His will. The God I was experiencing was relational, and in the world He created divine love is released in relationship, with Him and with His other creations. Like electricity jumping a gap from positive to negative, it requires two poles to flow. The relational God seemed to be, as my first sponsor Chuck once put it, "endlessly loving, endlessly forgiving, all powerful, and always having our best interest at heart." The hypothesis that this is God's nature has been proven to my satisfaction again and again over the years since I first became willing to consider Chuck's essentially Christian concept of God. It's not as if He is an old man with a beard, but it's as if the wisest, kindliest authority figure imaginable was looking over my life, giving me nudges and lifts to edge me toward a path – but only by my invitation, never imperiously.

This admixture of Zen and AA's underlying Christian concepts, grounded in my personal experiences with the divine, was the foundation for my beliefs about God when Alice entered my life a year and a half into sobriety. Within a few months she had heard my backstory and gone to a couple of open AA meetings with me. Alice knew that I believed in God, but not in Christianity or organized religion.

Alice grew up in the church and saw what happened to her family when her father left it. She told me that the man she would marry didn't have to believe in Christianity, but he had to go to church with her every Sunday. By then, I wanted to be the man she would marry, so I began going with her and her brothers to their childhood church.

It was awful. Her pastor was a legalist, certain that God had created a gnostic path to heaven open only to those who practiced the rituals perfectly. This boiled the elect down to basically his congregation and possibly a couple others like it, although those were questionable. The 2.3 billion members of other Christian denominations, the Buddhists, the nonbelievers, all my friends and family, Mother Theresa, Dietrich Bonhoeffer, Gandhi, were all doomed to eternal torment in a fiery hell.

The God I encountered through AA did not require legalistic confessions of faith. He ran to me when I was still agnostic and years away from considering Christianity. The loving God I had experienced seemed highly unlikely to send Presbyterians, gentle Zen Buddhists, and compassionate nonbelievers to eternal torment in a fiery hell.

To prepare to argue this point with Alice's preacher, I read the New Testament, underlining everything Jesus said about love, forgiveness, spirituality, the insignificance of and occasional perniciousness of religious ritual, the lightness of God's yoke, and the presence of God's kingdom all around us. I never had the argument with Alice's preacher I was preparing for – it would not have changed the pastor's convictions one iota – but studying the New Testament changed me. I realized that the Jesus I saw in the scriptures, not the hellfire God being preached, was laying out a spiritual path I was drawn to follow.

I discussed this with my Zen priest, noting all the trouble that people claiming to be Christian had wrought and expecting her to subtly agree. Instead, she cautioned: "Don't throw out the baby with the bathwater."

I finally recognized I had become Jesus' disciple one night after driving Alice home from a date. Earlier, when the elevator doors opened into the lobby of my co-op as we were leaving to drive back to Alice's mother's house, a clutch of boisterous drunken teenagers careened in. Edging past them, I heard a couple of the teens castigating a particularly sloppy boy for doing something particularly obnoxious. I didn't catch what it was, but I was familiar with most of the ways drunk teenage boys can be offensive, having been one in packs of others for many years. I didn't give it much thought.

When we pulled away from the curb to start the drive to Queens, Alice, who was born in Hong Kong, asked, "Did you hear what that kid said?" My hearing is poor and I admitted that I hadn't caught it. "He called me a gook." I won't recount my first thoughts in a book for my children, but suffice it to say I was outraged. How dare that insolent whelp disrespect my Alice! Probably deeper and unrecognized at the time, how dare that young man challenge me by insulting my girl in front of me? Alice was upset, but far less than me. Compared to the bias and physical perils she had faced for being Asian, including being chased out of Howard Beach by a mob as a kid, this was a minor slight from an insignificant source.

On the way back to Westchester after delivering Alice to her mother's house in Queens, I was still stewing over what to do. Where I came from, Clint Eastwood embodied the ideal for responding to attacks on your honor. What would Dirty Harry do in this situation? I had seen the kids push the elevator button for the floor below mine as we exited. I had a licensed Berretta 9mm pistol and two clips of jacketed hollow points in my apartment. When I got home, I could get my gun, go down a floor, find the noise from their party, and knock on the door. When they opened it, I would scare the daylights out of them. That would teach them not to insult my beloved.

Out of nowhere, I pictured Jesus, beaten, battered, and bent under the weight of His cross, being spat on and mocked by the Roman soldiers and the crowd lining the Via Dolorosa on His way up Calvary Hill. With all the power in the universe at his disposal, how did Jesus respond? Not with Eastwoodian vengeance. Jesus prayed to God to show mercy to his tormentors, asking in His extremis: "Father, forgive them, for they do not know what they are doing." I recalled how earlier in His ministry, Jesus had taught: "If someone slaps you on one cheek, turn to them the other also ... Do to others as you would have them do to you."

The anger, and the accompanying fear of the consequences that might follow if I feloniously confronted my perceived enemies, released like air from an untied balloon. I knew what my macho, redneck culture demanded in this situation, but a new hero, more powerful than any of my old models, set a radically different example – and I knew immediately that I would follow it. In that moment, I realized that I was looking to Jesus as my paradigm. I had become His follower. Without seeing it coming, I had become a Christian.

One of my Zen teachers, Joko Beck, taught that at some point we need to stop flitting from tradition to tradition and make a commitment to a spiritual practice. She used the imagery of closing the oven door and baking – following, without equivocation or retreat, the practice we've chosen so that its process of spiritual maturation can complete its transformative work on us. I knew I could not make a commitment to Buddhism. Zen meditation put me in a state to receive and acknowledge God's presence, but to go beyond Zen meditation practice and embrace its underlying Buddhism would require me to eventually commit to Buddhism's broader cosmology, and I wasn't buying into karma or reincarnation (I am not saying they aren't legitimate – how could I know that? – only that they did not resonate with me).

Early in my New Testament readings, I had reconciled Jesus' teachings with the loving divinity I often experienced in AA and sometimes encountered in Zen meditation, so I saw no inconsistency being a Christian who sat zazen or participated in AA. At the same time, I recognized from my readings how profoundly Christian grace differed from Buddhist karma, and Christian grace seemed more consistent with my experience. I have surely not gotten the life I deserve, thank God, and there have been issues, like my alcoholism, that needed more than my desire to do the right thing to escape.[4] I could commit to a religion premised on grace.

Beyond Christ's example and theology, one of Jesus' parables, the Parable of the Prodigal Son, shined like a diamond to me when I read the New Testament. It seemed a perfect abstract of my spiritual life seen from God's perspective. Jesus' parable confirmed that my experience of God's love and forgiveness was consistent with core Christianity. The parable goes like this:

There was a man who had two sons. The younger one said to his father, "Father, give me my share of the estate." So he divided his property between them. Not long after that, the younger son got together all he had, set off for a distant country and there squandered his wealth in wild living.

After he had spent everything, there was a severe famine in that whole country, and he began to be in need. So he went and hired himself out to a citizen of that country, who sent him to his fields to feed pigs. He longed to fill his stomach with the pods that the pigs were eating, but no one gave him anything.

When he came to his senses, he said, "How many of my father's hired servants have food to spare, and here I am starving to death! I will set out and go back to my father and say to him: Father, I have sinned against heaven and against you. I am no longer worthy to be called your son; make me like one of your hired servants." So he got up and went to his father.

But while he was still a long way off, his father saw him and was filled with compassion for him; he ran to his son, threw his arms around him and kissed him.

The son said to him, "Father, I have sinned against heaven and against you. I am no longer worthy to be called your son."

But the father said to his servants, "Quick! Bring the best robe and put it on him. Put a ring on his finger and sandals on his feet. Bring the fattened calf and kill it. Let's have a feast and celebrate. For this son of mine was dead and is alive again; he was lost and is found." So they began to celebrate.[5]

Like the younger son in Jesus' parable, as an angry teen I had taken all the gifts and talents the Father gave me, turned my back to God, and wasted my inheritance in an alien place far from where I belonged. There I ended up lost, enslaved, and miserable, wishing for the most basic emotional comfort that the lowest around me seemed to enjoy. The parable says God gave me free will to turn away from Him and to encounter the consequences of that choice, but the Divine Father never stopped loving me or hoping I would use my free will to turn back toward Him.

One day, beginning with the epiphany as my second wife left that there was something fundamentally and undeniably wrong with my life, and continuing into the conversation with Chuck and Ruari at my first AA meeting that finally shattered my cracking shell of denial, like the prodigal son in the parable, I came to my senses and saw where I was. I was an alcoholic who had lost the power to control my drinking and my life was spinning hopelessly out of control.

God knew exactly when this "moment of clarity," as it's called in AA, would arrive. He sent His servants Chuck and Ruari into my world three weeks before my first AA meeting, so that when I appeared on schedule at that meeting, they could steer me home to God.

Like the parable's prodigal son, I didn't initially think I could have the churchgoers' filial relationship to God. That was for others unlike me who were born into a relationship with Him, people like the kids in my Sunday school class who got it from the start and stayed loyal to their Heavenly Father while I went the other way. God's servants in AA did not seem born to the manor like the churchgoers. The people in AA had been as lost and as dirty as me. To me, they seemed to earn their place in the kingdom through sober service to their sovereign. It wasn't their birthright. A transactional relationship with God looked wonderful after believing that I would never have any relationship with Him. I would be happy if my Higher Power let me enjoy the emotional peace His servants in AA seemed to have in return for a life of service to Him.

Like the prodigal son, however, when I turned toward a Higher Power in prayer, still far from believing I might ever come home to live as God's beloved child, He ran to me, stroked my back as I lay on my futon, shooed my fears and unshackled me from the addiction to alcohol and drugs that was destroying my life. I would serve my Father, but from love and gratitude, not as consideration for His beneficence, which required only my willingness to accept it.

Later, like the lost son in the parable, I made my confessions. Through the AA steps, I looked at my life and admitted to God all the ways I had failed Him. Like the father in the parable, God forgave everything. God welcomed me home as a lost son found, with a celebration that continues to this day, showering me with gifts: my AA community, Alice, our kids, our home, our friends, our church community, my career, restored relationships with my parents and siblings, and so much more.

The parable helped confirm Jesus' divinity for me. How else could Jesus have a God's-eye view of my life story twenty centuries before I lived it? Jesus' parable put my story in context as part of the infinitely broader story of

God's timeless, perennial grace: a story where, as Dr. King put it in paraphrase of abolitionist preacher Theodore Parker's 1853 sermon, "The arc of the moral universe is long, but it bends toward justice." It's a good story to be part of.

I realized that night in the car, driving home from Queens to Westchester, that Jesus had become my rabbi. His example and his teachings had become my polestar, illuminating my place in God's firmament and my path through the world. For me, Jesus had a spiritual authority, confirmed by my experiences, above any other source. That meant, I supposed, that I was now a Christian and Christianity would be the oven I baked in.

While accepting the fundamental Christian premise that Jesus as God made incarnate is the epitome of what a human seeking God should strive to imitate, I don't pray to Jesus or directly worship Him as many Christians do. Rather, I see Jesus' teachings and example as what the Buddhists describe authentic religion to be – a finger pointing at the moon. "Don't stare at the finger," they caution, "look at the moon!"[6]

Jesus pointed me to a loving God like the one I had seen in AA and showed me how a godly man seeking to enact God's will ought to behave. The rich depth of Christianity has been enormously important in my life, especially as I see the road home Christianity describes in metaphor laid out for me. God sent His devoted servant Alice to bring me to Christianity, along with countless other good things. Christianity was the last place I planned to go, but I would have followed Alice anywhere.

There is a huge variance in Christian practice across denominations and, with congregational churches like we have always attended, from congregation to congregation within the denomination. In the churches we favor, there can be a range of individual belief even among that church's congregants.

Over the years, we migrated to churches that preached the radically inclusive gospel we saw in the scriptures. To the extent that the vision of Christianity I see preached in a church is consistent with my experience with God and with what Jesus said and did, I accept it. I have not seen any evidence of the wrathful God who struck down the firstborn of Egypt, incinerated Sodom and Gomorrah, and ordered the Israelites to "kill everything that breathes" in some enemies' cities,[7] but Jesus speaks often of a God like the one in his parable that I've experienced – the merciful, loving, forgiving God. I go to churches that worship that God.

In considering a God consistent with my experience, I am uncomfortable with Christian exclusivity. I have felt God's presence and love in the stillness of the zendo and there are Zen koans that, like Jesus' parables, seem to hold wisdom beyond mortals', touching off a flash of illumination that allows me to see and appreciate God's hand in my life. God conveys His will to me most consistently in AA meetings, where life's mundane challenges are reset in a spiritual context. Christianity provides the architect's blueprint for my life, while AA shows me how to build that life board by board from the rough materials of my daily struggles.

In sum, the God whose work I have seen seems to find many paths to reach us, and then to draw us to Him.[8] He happens to have called me to Christianity.

THE GIRL ON THE TRAIN

When the doubts creep in, my faith dims, and the concept of an omnipotent God starts to feel like a myth again, this is the day I return to. It stands in defiance of any mental argument that the world is operating randomly, without divine purpose or intervention. I promise that everything I'm about to say about that day is true to the best of my recollection.

Three years before my touchstone encounter with God's handiwork on the train, I was reeling from my first wife's departure. A college sweetheart, she was attractive and worked for a company that booked high level investors' conferences. I had been faithful but not much of a husband otherwise. Most of my energy went into my addictions. She took up with a French businessman and decamped for Paris while I was on a business trip. I came home to her yellow sticky departure notice on the bathroom mirror and two rings on the sink. It was dramatic, but not unjustified. I promised to love her and I consistently broke that promise. I was incapable of keeping it. My parents taught me that an unloved wife must endure in the marriage. My first wife taught me that she doesn't.

When she left, I felt, as I always felt toward the end of a relationship, that no woman would ever want me again. In sobriety, I would be able to dig down to a root fear that I was unlovable and would eventually be abandoned by anyone I loved. The fear wasn't rational, of course, it was just there. I imagine now that it had something to do with the ice age that overcame what had been a warm childhood when my doting older sisters left for college just as my dad's nascent affair wrecked the intimacy of my parents' marriage. Whatever. As always happened at the end of a relationship, when my first wife left I was desperate to find another woman who would love me, a sacrifice to the god of my insecurities.

A former girlfriend of one of my fraternity brothers worked in an entry level position for a client of my firm. We'll call her Kate. She was lost and lonely in the big city. I had a couple meals with her, being as charming as I could to try to prove to myself that I could still attract someone, and the attention worked. Lonely as she was, she developed a crush on me and announced it one night in the lobby of a hotel where we had dinner. That was all I needed. She was a nice person but I had no real interest in her. I never spoke to her again.

I am as repelled by my selfishness now as you probably are, but as Dr. Karl Menninger put it, an alcoholic or addict is like a person on fire who runs into the ocean and drowns. They don't care who they bowl over as they run to the water. They just want out of their unbearable pain.

AA similarly takes the view that when we are enslaved by addiction, we are often blind to our selfishness and unable to stop ourselves from hurting people. In sobriety, we have the ability and the duty to try to make amends for our harms. As we do that, we should be guided by a mentor, called a sponsor, who can help us to not cause fresh harm through the amends process to people we have already hurt. When we came to my amends, my sponsor forbade me from contacting old flames on the premise that I had inflicted enough pain, we were young, they had probably moved on and would be best left alone. If God thought they needed to see me, my sponsor assured me, God would arrange for us to meet and I could apologize then. In the meantime, I could make a more general amends by treating the women around me with kindness and respect.

Three years after leaving Kate in the hotel lobby and newly sober, I waited at my station for my regular morning train to the city. As any rail commuter knows, there is a trial and error process of identifying the best spot to stand on the station platform so that when the train comes you will be directly in front of the door to the car with more empty seats at your stop than the other cars, or the car that will best position you to avoid stairwell congestion when you exit. Since my commute from Westchester County to Manhattan was over forty minutes, I focused on seats instead of exit position. Over the years, I arrived at the optimal spot on my home station platform to wait for the inbound train. Triangulating off landmarks, I positioned myself within six inches of the same spot every weekday morning to enter first into the best car for seats.

That clear winter morning three months after I quit drinking, I stepped through the train door that opened in front of my appointed spot and, to my delight, saw empty seats. Then, I did something I cannot explain. Instead of quickly grabbing a seat before the passengers filing in behind me filled all of them, for no rational reason and with no thought as to why I should do it, I ignored the empty seats in my regular car and, as the train eased away from the station, walked forward into the next car. There were still a few empty seats in that car too. Again, for no reason and with no thought about why I was doing it, I walked forward through that car to the next car, and then the next. There was a smattering of open seats scattered throughout that car's three-across rows. As the train pulled into the next stop, I took an aisle seat. The middle seats fill last and the one to my left was vacant.

There's an art to seat guarding, if you are so inclined, and at that point in life, I was. I opened my *New York Times* and assiduously avoided eye contact with the passengers boarding at the station after mine. If a passenger walking down the aisle scouting seats had to get my attention, it made it harder for them to ask me to stand and allow them into the middle seat than if I looked up at them and made eye contact. That was practically an invitation for them to intrude on my space. I considered it a guilty victory when the passengers filled other middle seats and the one next to me stayed vacant after the first stop.

There was one more station stop before the train ran express to Grand Central Station. It was a long shot, but if I could feign enough immersion in the *Times* to deter the passengers boarding there from disturbing me, there was a slight chance that the middle seat next to me would stay empty for the rest of the ride. That would be a big day. I opened the paper wide to make it harder for the other passengers to see my face.

The train came to a stop at the second station after mine with a hiss of air brakes. The pneumatic doors slid open. I held the paper high and stared at it with what I hoped was a look of deep concentration. It would be a sin to rouse me from such intense thought, but I was roused nonetheless. As the last of the open seats in the car filled, someone tapped me on the shoulder and asked if she could sit in the middle seat next to me. With a sigh of mild exasperation, I stood, still staring at the paper to confirm that my rapt interest in the article I was pretending to read was not a charade, then sat back down without looking at the face of the intruder settling in beside me.

I had noticed, as I peeked below the paper at the person sliding in front of me to enter the middle seat, that it was a young woman. After we both sat down, I stole a glance sideways to see if she was at least pretty. It was Kate.

I had enough AA in me to recognize that I could not ignore her for the rest of the ride and caught her attention. She had not seen that it was me hiding behind the paper. Since the morning train can be quiet enough that all the surrounding passengers overhear a conversation, we stayed with light small talk. Did she live in the town where she boarded the train? No, she was visiting a girlfriend. She had never been on this train line before. She seemed happier than she had been when I had known her years before.

After we exited at Grand Central, I apologized for treating her so poorly, explaining that it had nothing to do with her. I had been struggling with addiction and divorce but was getting help now. It wasn't a great amends at that early stage and without my sponsor's oversight in planning it, but she seemed grateful for the encounter. She said it was OK, and it seemed like it was. I haven't seen her again. Over the years, I had one-time chance meetings like this with two other women I dated. It seems that my ex-flames were much less devastated by my departure than I imagined they would be.

That evening, at home after work with time to reflect, the full significance of this encounter sunk in. Something I couldn't explain made me deviate from my ironclad habit of always taking the first open aisle or window seat in my customary car. (My family knows how decades later that trait remains strong. I will grab an open parking spot two blocks away from our house in Brooklyn rather than continuing on, as Matthew or Alice would, to see if there might be a spot closer to home.) Then, whatever broke me out of my pattern spurred me to walk forward through first one and then a second car into yet another car, where I passed up several empty seats to choose the one I ended up in. Then, the middle seat next to me stayed open as the train filled at the first station after mine. All this happened so that when the train stopped at the second station after mine, I was on the right train, in the right car, in the right seat, near the right door (there are two in each car) for Kate – who would only ride this train once – to enter, turn left instead of right, and without seeing that it was me, choose my row to sit in.

The probability of all these events lining up by chance is too remote to enter the realm of possibility. Chance will never let this happen. It cannot be coincidental. Something *made* this happen. And whatever it was that made this happen, it was able to control both Kate and me, without our knowing it, and it could move forward and backward and across time and space to put us on separate paths toward an ultimate intersection. Presumably we were not its sole focus that day. Presumably millions or billions of other synchronicities were being managed simultaneously. I cannot imagine, much less understand, something that could do this. Whether I can understand it or not, it clearly is and it clearly can.

The girl on the train is my rally point when my belief in the divine erodes. I have seen something mysterious, beyond my ability to imagine or understand, manipulate events and people across time and space to create outcomes that ultimately seem elegant, loving, and healing. The easiest thing to call this mysterious force is God, since that's what other people call it, but I try to use that word without all the freight that sometimes attaches to it. I am talking about the God of my experience.

THE DRUNK ON THE TRAIN

I had another divine encounter on a commuter train ten years later. I will tell you about the graceful way Alice and I met in a bit, but by this time we were married and living in Princeton, New Jersey. Alice was in graduate school in Philadelphia and I still worked in New York. In earlier times, Princeton was the stagecoach stop between New York and Philadelphia, a day's ride from each. It wasn't a day's ride from either city on New Jersey Transit, but it was an hour on the train.

Having been a rail commuter for over a decade by then, I used the train ride from Princeton Junction to New York to catch up on my correspondence or to edit a brief. On the way home, I did more of the same or decompressed with a book. Friday nights were reserved for a crossword or a book to transition into the weekend and leave the stresses of the job in the city until Monday.

This Friday night was a good one. I had a window seat facing northwest. It was early fall and still light as we emerged out of the Hudson River tunnel into the industrial New Jersey wetlands. I dipped in and out of my book, alternating reading with gazing out at the tranquil early evening sky, my mind wandering, processing the hectic week. The car was quiet, with only occasional murmurs of conversation, too far from me to be drawn into them. Perfect.

Until the Newark stop, that is. I sensed a disturbance in the Force behind me almost immediately as we pulled away from the station. The trains had high-backed seats and I was slouched down with my knees braced against the seat ahead of me, so it would have taken a major reorganization to pop up like a prairie dog and survey what was going on back there. Turning would also risk eye contact that would draw me into engagement with what I quickly identified as the source of the unrest, a noisy drunk who had boarded in Newark and was bumping his way down the aisle.

As fate would have it, he crash-landed into the window seat directly behind mine. The other passengers in that row quickly dispersed. Before long, as the drunk ranted, the other passengers in my row moved away too. I thought about moving but stayed put, hunkered down lower, and tried unsuccessfully to read. I prayed that the train's motion didn't make the drunk puke and kept an ear tuned for the first sign of retching, hoping I might spring clear of the expulsion.

After a while, I gave up trying to read and listened to what the drunk was saying to us, taking it as an unpleasant anthropology lesson. The rest of the train was now dead silent, on edge, waiting to see what the drunk would do.

I suppose that having spent so much time around drunks when I was one, I have more experience than most people in deciphering slurred speech. It took a while, but eventually I realized that the urgency in the drunk's voice was not hostility toward the rest of us – he was frightened. He had to change trains in Trenton for the SEPTA train to Philadelphia. He didn't know how he was going to do it.

I realized that I been as drunk as he was in other transit situations, and it had been terrifying. You knew that you had to remember to do something at some point, but you couldn't hold on to the thought of what it was or how to do it. I was still on edge thinking that the drunk would puke or turn violent – I knew from hard experience that drunks are mercurial – but now I also felt compassion. He was afraid. That's all.

The drunk kept cycling on the Trenton transfer, mournfully asking again and again how he would do it. No one answered. Finally, there was another voice in the silence of the clicking car – mine.

"It's easy," I said evenly, without turning around. "When you get to Trenton, ask the conductor where to get the Philly train. He will point you to it. You can't go wrong."

This seemed to calm him for a minute, but he couldn't retain the information. We had the same exchange at least four times. Finally, he was quiet for a few minutes. Maybe it had sunk in.

I heard him trying to strike a match.

"You can't smoke on the train," I said. "The conductor will call the cops and they will take you off the train." After a couple repetitions, he stopped trying to strike the match. We were in New Brunswick now, twenty minutes out from Princeton Junction.

A few minutes later, we repeated the exchange about the transfer in Trenton. He announced that he didn't know about tickets.

"You'll have to buy a ticket in Trenton," I said, imposing another insurmountable complication on the drunk. I told him he could get one at a window or at a machine, but I knew that for someone in the drunk's condition, that would be an unimaginably complex operation. He knew it too and began to bewail the impossibility of it.

"It will cost you more," I said, still facing forward in my seat, not turning around, "but you can buy a ticket on the train." That must have seemed doable, and he fell silent again. The train clicked on, taking forever to reach my station.

A few minutes later, I gathered from his loud muttering that the drunk could not figure out whether he had enough money for the ticket to Philadelphia. I looked out the window. It was getting dark and I saw my own face in the reflection. We were less than ten minutes from my stop. There was no getting around it. I had to engage, but at least my escape was imminent. I unspooled, stood up, and moved to the aisle seat in the drunk's emptied row.

It was the first time I looked at him. He was bleary and swaying, unable to focus on me. He was really drunk and looked like he'd been that way for a while, with a two-day shadow and mussed hair. He looked like he had fallen, from the evidence on his pants knees, but he didn't appear to be living on the street. He seemed more like a marginally employed man on a serious bender, misplaced among the executives commuting home from New York.

"How much money do you have?" I asked.

He reached into his pockets and held out a passel of crumpled bills and coins to me in both hands, a supplicant trying unsuccessfully to concentrate on our exchange. I counted his money.

"You have enough," I told him. "Just ask the conductor in Trenton where to get on the Philly train. You can buy a ticket from the conductor on the Philly train."

He seemed to comprehend.

"Put the money away," I said, knowing that he could easily misplace it after I left. He smiled wanly and stuffed the money back in his dirty jeans. I returned to my seat and checked our progress out the window. Only five minutes from Princeton Junction. If he didn't puke or engage with me again, the threat and embarrassment of our public discourse would all be over soon. I packed my unread book in my briefcase, put on my suit jacket, and slid to the aisle seat.

As the train rocked gently forward, I knew there was one more thing to do. I pulled out my address book (no smartphones then) and looked up the number for AA's Intergroup office. I tore a corner off a legal pad sheet in my briefcase and wrote down the words "AA Meetings" and the AA Intergroup number. If he called it, Intergroup could give him the time and address of meetings near wherever he was. Then, beneath that, in block letters I wrote, "BOB L" and my phone number.

Coat on, briefcase in hand, I waited until the train was no more than two minutes from my station but before the departing passengers filled the aisle, and moved back to the aisle seat behind me again. The drunk looked at me, still unfocused. It was dark outside now, with just the train lights on us. There was no outside anymore, just us inside.

"Look," I said, holding the note out to him. He took it and stared at it, too drunk to read.

"That has the number for AA," I said. "If you ever get tired of drinking, you call that number, OK? They will tell you how to get connected with AA." He seemed to possibly understand what I was saying. He kept trying to focus on me, looking at me silently.

"It's got my number on it too," I added quietly. "If you want to stop drinking, you can call me, anytime. I used to drink too," I said. He continued looking at me, trying to focus.

"Put that in your pocket," I said, and he did.

The passengers were beginning to stand and move down the aisle toward the door, studiously avoiding eye contact with the drunk. I stood and joined them, without looking back at him. I had done what I needed to. There was a sense of relief. We were finished and he hadn't puked on me.

Someone on the line for the door said, "You were really good with that guy. I wouldn't have known what to do."

"I've been that drunk on a train," I said. "He's just frightened."

The person who spoke to me seemed to regret having done so and turned back to study the door. We all clicked on in silence as the train blessedly began to slow for our stop. Almost there.

"Mr. Man!" the drunk said loudly. I ignored him. He yelled it again, louder. No one turned but me.

"Am I Mr. Man?" I asked him. He nodded and beckoned me to him. I walked back to the aisle seat and leaned in.

"I used to go to AA too," he said.

"Come back," I said, the words coming through me now, not from my head. "We want you back." I meant it, and he knew it. The embarrassment was gone and I felt nothing but compassion for him. We were brothers.

And then, in an instant, the drunk was gone. It's hard to describe. There wasn't a drunk in the seat. There was something else, otherworldly, not so much seen as perceived. It was a bright, soft radiance, pure love filling me.

The train was stopping. I turned away and left the car without looking back. I was sure that by now the drunk had returned and the radiance was gone, but for a moment I, alone among all the passengers on the train, had been in the unmistakable presence of God.

"Then the King will say to those on his right, 'Come, you who are blessed by my Father; take your inheritance, the kingdom prepared for you since the creation of the world. For I was hungry and you gave me something to eat, I was thirsty and you gave me something to drink, I was a stranger and you

43

invited me in, I needed clothes and you clothed me, I was sick and you looked after me, I was in prison and you came to visit me.'

"Then the righteous will answer him, 'Lord, when did we see you hungry and feed you, or thirsty and give you something to drink? When did we see you a stranger and invite you in, or needing clothes and clothe you? When did we see you sick or in prison and go to visit you?'

"The King will reply, 'Truly I tell you, whatever you did for one of the least of these brothers and sisters of mine, you did for me.'[9]

I don't know how righteous I am, but I have no doubt that God did appear on New Jersey Transit that night. Jesus' story at least gives me a way to talk about it with other Christians who may not have had the same experience, with the authority of scripture to suggest that perhaps I didn't imagine it. Scripture is good for that.

A GHOST STORY

To the extent that prophets thought to have insight into God's nature describe a loving God consistent with the mysterious divinity I have experienced, I am sometimes able to trust their further assurance that there is more to us than our bodies; we have a transcendent spiritual nature which survives our inevitable physical decay. Put more simply, I can believe that we are spiritual beings having a human existence. A favorite Eastern metaphor is that we come from a source and pass our life like drops of water in a waterfall, reuniting, after our brief separation, with the source.

The hope of an afterlife of the spirit is hugely reassuring as my physical life nears its end. As usual, however, I must overcome a scientific skeptic's doubts to accept it. Here is my empirical experience of the world beyond ours, which I fall back on when doubt won't allow me to take what others say about an afterlife on faith.

One Sunday in late winter when Alice and I lived in New Jersey, we had lunch with our pastor and his wife. They were Texans, sent north from the southern seat of the denomination we then attended to bring light into the Yankee darkness. The best and the worst of that denomination was its deep, fundamentalist view of the primacy of the New Testament Bible. At best, that guiding principle engaged its members directly with the text, which is powerful. At worst, it papered over the Bible's inconsistencies, storytelling conventions, and ancient Middle Eastern context to read scripture as a timeless codification of divinely ordained rules.

The big issue of the day in that denomination was women's role in the church. That alone should tell you how far from Jesus they had wandered. Traditionally, most churches in the denomination took the direction attributed to the Apostle Paul that women should remain silent in the temple literally.[10] In those churches, women could not preach or otherwise lead worship from the front of the auditorium (although inconsistently, they could sing from the back). The congregations recognized that inequitable treatment was at odds with women's role in the national culture, but they saw Paul's dictum as an edict that God had pronounced through Paul. We might not understand it, but it was not ours to question God's wisdom.

A few congregations of that denomination, like the one where I was baptized and married, saw the verses as advice from Paul (or later Pauline followers, according to some historians) not to engage in practices that the broad, egalitarian freedom of Christ's teachings permitted when those practices would so offend the dominant culture that their use kept people from hearing the good news of Christ's gospel. That interpretation reasoned that a woman speaking in a first-century Jewish temple would be such a scandalous departure from traditional religious customs that exercising her new Christian equality would overshadow Jesus' message. Seen in that contextual light, a congregation not allowing women a full role in worship in late twentieth century America was exactly the sort of needless cultural affront Paul counseled against.[11]

The New Jersey preacher knew that Alice and I were strongly on the latter side of that debate, but he felt that reassessing women's roles was too potentially divisive to consider publicly with the congregation. It was easier just to go along so that the more traditional element would not be offended. Even now I feel my blood rising over what I saw as un-Christian conciliation with a fundamentally wrong position. Because of our theological divide on this issue, our relationship with the pastor and his wife was strained.

When they invited us to lunch that day, we were grateful for the hospitality, but the atmosphere was a little tense as we carefully sidestepped the minefield of our doctrinal differences. This made it particularly surprising when the pastor's wife, an ebullient, teased-blonde Texas farmgirl, started talking about the ghosts in their house. The pastor was visibly uncomfortable that she would expose a secret to us which could undermine their credibility in these foreign mission fields; but she had come with him to the frigid north, this was weighing heavily on her mind, and she was not a gal who was going to keep an upsetting development to herself. Sheepishly, the pastor agreed that what she was saying about the ghosts was true.

They told us that their old house was commissioned as a field hospital during the Revolutionary War's Battle of Princeton. They had noises in the attic rising to the level of a keg party, lights turning on and off, perceptions of cold presences, objects flying across the room.

Alice and I had experienced similar perceptions. Alice lived in a house growing up that the family thought haunted, and we spent a night in my sister's seventeenth-century New England farmhouse which led us to agree with her belief that her home was haunted. In Princeton, while house hunting, we walked into one of the dozens of places we looked at, immediately and independently felt a dark presence, looked at each other, and said, "Do you feel that too?" We confirmed that we both felt it, told the realtor the house wasn't for us, and quickly skedaddled.

Our pastor downplayed mysticism and went to great lengths to try to align Christianity with science. For him to confirm experiencing otherworldly visitations was a bit chilling. As he noted at lunch, the Bible describes a spiritual world inhabited by angels, demons, and ghosts, but I like a more ordered, comprehensible world, where the only spiritual entities are divine love in its various forms opposed – but never vanquished – by evil.

I was thinking about all this later that day as I drove through upstate New York for a deposition in Utica the next morning. By the time I reached the New York State Thruway, the weather had turned and there was no time to think about anything but trying to stay alive as flurries collapsed into a blizzard. The passing lane became accessible only across a slippery mound of snow that waggled the car's tail too disturbingly to cross. I grew up in snow country and knew how quickly a car can go out of control on roads like this. For the last twenty miles, the passing lane was closed off and we slogged through the storm single file in the dark at thirty miles per hour, praying no one stopped suddenly in front of us or more slowly behind us.

Finally, I reached Utica and traversed the sad, snowy downtown to a budget motel with low watt lights and a noisy under-window heater. Having been sober long enough to know that I would I not be tempted by the taps at the only open restaurant I could reach on foot, I walked to a working man's tavern down the street for a hamburger, then padded back through the snow to the hotel and tucked in.

I lay in the bed, eyes open. Streetlights reflected off the snowy streets, backlighting the window shade and casting soft shadows across the room. The snow was still falling. I tried to relax after the white-knuckle drive. My mind returned to the lunch conversation. I was troubled at how the preacher had reluctantly confirmed our suspicions that the spiritual realm was astir with spirits beyond the loving God and the cold evil I knew from experience.

And then, before I fell asleep, in the mottled semi-darkness of that sad hotel in that half-abandoned town, I felt my mother's presence.

My mother died a few months before, after a horrific crossing. Progressive Supranuclear Palsy, a rare and nastier cousin of Lou Gehrig's Disease, spent five years eroding her muscle control. First, she lost her balance and began to fall forward. In one fall, she broke her hip and lay on the floor for hours before my father came home to find her. Then, she began to lose fine motor control in her fingers, then all motor control. She lost control of her bowels and bladder. Worst of all, she lost the ability to speak, becoming more and more incomprehensible. One of the last things she said that we understood, deciphered only after hours of her fighting to make herself understood, was "Kill me." She remained trapped in silence for two more years after that, with only partial control over one finger.

I was sober when she got sick and managed to show up for her occasionally at my parents' retirement home in Mobile, Alabama. Near the end, I sat by her bed listening to her fight for air, praying that God would let her pass, taking hope in the silence between breaths that my prayer had been answered, only to hear her begin fighting for another breath. After a while, I changed my prayer to simply asking that God's will be done. It was the beginning of learning that when I pray like God works for me, I grow tense and frustrated and my faith dims if God does not immediately respond by doing what I ask. When I pray like I work for God, asking God for acceptance and to be shown how to serve and empowered to do so, I relax and feel God's grace around me.

Perhaps my greatest service to my mother came near the end. Our family had gathered in Mobile. Mom was in the hospital, in and out of consciousness. She had pneumonia. Her neurologist came into the room where her five children waited and told us that we were at a crossroads. The hospital could treat the pneumonia with antibiotics, and she might recover from it, or they could not administer antibiotics and move our mother to hospice, where she would be made comfortable. There was a stunned silence. My father did not step in. His devotion to my mother's needs during her illness notwithstanding, his counsel on whether to let my mother die was too compromised by his ongoing affair to be accepted by his daughters. Words came through me, not my own: "Doctor, are you telling us that if we treat the pneumonia we may be interfering with the agent God sent to end our mother's suffering and bring her home?" A sister doubled over with a spontaneous moan. We all knew what to do.

My relationship with my mother was tangled with threads of guilt and distance, complicated by a feeling, from long before she got sick, that her fear had infected me and her neediness would suffocate me if I came too close. I remember her warm comfort when we were young and the family bubbled with joy, but in my teens that all ended. My dad lost his parents and began his affair with a much younger co-worker that continued the rest of his life, culminating in marriage after my mother died. My older siblings left for college and boarding school. The usual teenage rebelliousness was further stoked by the generational schisms of the 1960s between the World War II generation and the disenchanted Vietnam War generation.

In my case, the distancing was multiplied by having to hide my habits. I started smoking in seventh grade and had to keep a physical distance from my mother so she wouldn't smell the smoke on me. I had to sneak out for a cigarette in the evening. I was drinking on weekends and had to lie about that. I was experimenting with drugs that were still highly taboo. I had to lie to my mother continually to cover my tracks and I had to stay away from the house as much as possible. Once I started college, I rarely came home, and when I did, I was mostly out with my friends.

I blamed my mother for the tension in our family. There was a summer when she wouldn't speak to my dad at all. We sat in taut silence through family dinners, punctuated at best by a brief eddy of conversation across the table that never included both ends, my paper napkin nervously shredding to bits under the table. I almost believed my father when he said that he only started the affair after my mother had wrongly accused him of cheating for so long that he figured if he was already doing the time, he might as well do the crime. Then, once my mother's health began to fail, it was excruciating to watch her suffering. In all, my relationship with my mother was predominantly a sad and disappointing mess, so damaged by the time I got sober that it could not be repaired before she became sick and silent, although I was a better son during that time.

When I felt my mother's presence that night in the Utica motel room, all of that was gone – all the neediness and sadness and sickness and guilt and fear and anger – hers and mine. I couldn't quite see her, but I could feel her soft, loving gaze. There was a gentle glow – not visible in the room but experienced around her. The pinched-in bitterness of her resentment toward my father was gone. There was no jealously where she was, no disappointment. There was only love. She was completely at peace in a broad sea of pure, selfless, sustaining love. I had the sense that if her unspeakable suffering for those last years was the refiner's fire that purified her so that she could be where she was for a timeless eternity, it was worth it all.

In that presence, all the damage I had caused to our relationship was gone, forgotten and with no price in guilt to be paid. My mother, in some form, just smiled her warm, perfect, mother's contented love on me and it warmed my soul. And then, after less than a minute, she faded out of my perception. I was alone in my hotel room but changed forever.

I realized that the conversation earlier in the day with the pastor helped me accept the possibility that, even in a monotheistic Christian cosmology, spiritual visitations like this had been recorded and accepted. That thought helped the peace settle into my deepest parts without my having to challenge it as irreligious. As I near the end of my life, I take immeasurable comfort from the glimpse of the afterlife my loving mother brought to me.

And then, a few months ago, struggling with a terminal diagnosis, I chanced into a conversation with my friend Kieran about his cousin's near-death experience which reinforced the vision my mother gave me.

Kieran's cousin was in a car accident, died, and was revived. Kieran had not heard my description of the vision my mother brought me, but his cousin had described being in a place exactly as I had glimpsed it – the sea of pure love, the lightness, the unblemished love of his late mother, who asked him if he was ready and released him back to earthly consciousness when he said no, he had work left to do. His cousin, Kieran said, had been a new man after that, and a far better one. And then a few days after that, my friend Dion told me about talking with a friend of his who had been dead from a massive stroke until revived. Dion's friend described the place he had seen similarly.

Thanks to a recommendation from Dale Pauls, the pastor who baptized me and married Alice and me, I read the seminal 1975 study of near-death experiences, *Life After Life*, by Raymond A. Moody, Jr, M.D. Distilling the otherworldly experiences of scores of people who were clinically dead and then revived, Moody describes survivors' common impressions as consistent with the three "white light" experiences I had: the night I prayed to the rug and my compulsion to drink was lifted, the drunk on the New Jersey Transit train who morphed into a vision of the divine, and the glimpse of the afterlife my mother gave me.

Acknowledging the vexing inadequacy of words to fully describe their experiences in a realm outside anything for which we have a shared lexicon, survivors told Moody about a feeling of peace, tranquility, comfort, and relief surpassing anything they had known. They experienced the loving presence of people who died before them, but not in physical form, just as I experienced my mother's presence in a way unlike any other. As one survivor of a near-death experience put it, obviously struggling with words: "I had the feeling that [a dead friend] was standing there, right next to me. I could see him in my mind and felt like he was there, but it was strange. I didn't see him in his physical body. I could see things, but not in physical form, yet just as clearly, his looks, everything." That is as about as close as I could come to articulating how I experienced my mother's presence, and the words still fail to capture it.

Moody says survivors offered an "utterly invariable" description of something he calls "the being of light," which survivors reported irrespective of their religious beliefs. It was an entity, with a personality, that has a "white" or "clear" light of "unearthly brilliance" which "doesn't dazzle or hurt the eyes." This sounds like the white light that enveloped my three encounters, a singular and unearthly light that slows time into the eternal when it appears.

Survivors told Moody that the being of light emanates "love and warmth ... utterly beyond words, and [the survivor] feels completely surrounded by it and taken up in it, completely at ease and accepted in the presence of this being. He senses an irresistible attraction to the light. He is ineluctably drawn to it." I could use these words to describe the presence that stroked my back and took away all my anxiety the night I first prayed, or that softly shown its love on me in the moment the drunk dissolved into something otherworldly on the commuter train, or the enveloping "love and warmth ... utterly beyond words" I felt in the glimpse of the afterlife my mother brought me.

An AA friend, an intellectually tough bestselling non-fiction author, died and was revived after an experience somewhat consistent with those Moody describes, but – she hastens to point out – without the "being of light." Instead, she perceived that perfect place as more akin to my moment of transcendence in the zendo: a sense of complete and blissful unity with the universe. I'd take that too.

As Moody acknowledges in his book, there are theories that the failing brain tricks dying people into hallucinating these experiences. Scientists are only permitted to postulate explanations consistent with natural law, reducing everything to a brick-by-brick extension of the known, unless they have the rare humility and courage, like Moody, to allow for the possibility of a supernatural explanation that humans will never fully understand. Science often leads us away from error toward the truth, but its inherent limitations sometimes obscure the truth. Science cannot abide deep mystery. Like some bystanders who Moody notes were caught up in and shared survivors' visions, I wasn't near death when I experienced the same inexpressible love, peace, light and warmth described by those who died and were revived. The bystanders and my impressions were not formed by oxygen starvation. We were breathing just fine. Any "scientific" explanation for my transcendent experiences rings hollow.

Moody's accounts of near-death experiences confirm and reinforce my belief that there is a spiritual realm waiting for me on the other side of this life and it will be wondrous beyond imagination. While I dread the physical experience of mortal illness and its impact on my loved ones, I am not afraid of death. I see it as a return to my spiritual home after this brief sojourn in a human body in the material realm. From everything I have seen of it, the place I will go to is the place my soul has longed for since I first became aware.

For many years, without thinking about it, I adopted two lines from a poem Dylan Thomas wrote to his dying father as the paradigm for how I should react to the inevitable physical decline of aging:

Do not go gentle into that good night.
Rage, rage against the dying of the light.

Recently, I read that Dylan Thomas died of alcoholism at thirty-nine. He didn't know the first thing about old age. And the great man's reported last words? "I've had eighteen straight whiskies, I think that's the record ..." This is the oracle I allowed to guide my thinking on old age and death? Do I want what he had? And isn't a basic tenet of the Twelve Steps that as a recovering alcoholic I have forfeited the right to rage against *anything*?[12]

Why should I not go gently, peacefully, into the Light? Why would I rage against that fate?

When I first got a terminal diagnosis, before the medicine paused the disease's progress to put more sand in my hourglass, I could sometimes sense that place of peace ahead of me. It's not like I was there in its cleansing light, but I could feel its glow on the horizon, like distant city lights on a dark highway. I felt like that glow is where I'm going, and I'm getting closer. When the medicine paused the process that was bringing me home to that light, I stopped sensing the light ahead of me.

I expect that when the medicine stops working, I may begin to feel the light ahead of me again as the cancer starts bringing me toward it once more. In the meantime, there is work to do here. I have a family to love and a story to tell.

THE ANGEL IN THE DELIVERY ROOM

I have told how I twice found myself in God's direct presence. I told how I found myself in my mother's spiritual essence. Another type of spiritual encounter happens much more frequently, sometimes several times in a year. These encounters might be called angelic, if we can use that term in the most general way without descending into a biblical exegesis of the qualities and hierarchies of angels and how many will fit on the head of a pin. The angels I'm talking about don't have wings or halos. They are mostly mortal except for those moments when immortality pulses through them to transmit God's love to someone in need. I'll call them part-time angels. God has used me as a part-time angel and if you're the type of person who reads things like this, I'd bet He has used you as one too.

When it happens, it's like you're a lightning rod struck by a pulse of supernatural love and wisdom that passes through you and is gone, leaving you as inert and incapable of generating that love and wisdom on your own as a lightning rod is of generating lightning. Maybe God inspired the bellman in Richmond to be the angel who would see me through a fragile point of early sobriety. Maybe I was an angel for the drunk on the train. When I have been a lightning rod that God used to transmit His message to someone in need, the spiritual power surge made me say things I would never naturally say and do things I would never naturally do.

Once the lightning struck while I leaned over the trunk of a rental car in a far corner of the parking lot of an Atlanta airport hotel, reaching for my bags. As I bumped them out of the trunk, I started at a voice behind me. I hadn't seen anyone else in the parking lot. The voice behind me said: "I need some money." I lowered my bags to the ground and turned around to see a rail-thin crackhead vibrating like a tuning fork three feet from me. "Gimme some money!" he said more aggressively, pill-rolling his fingers and taking a step closer.

Without any thought as to what I should do, I released the handles of my bags, stood up straight, and looked the crackhead in the face. I was being robbed. The physical threat should have flooded me with adrenaline and left me momentarily paralyzed, debating fight or flight options at hyperspeed. It didn't. Something short-circuited that instinct and instead of fear, I felt compassion.

I am definitely not the type of guy to feel love in a situation like this. I would expect myself to freeze or run or, if I was still carrying the Berretta, slide a hand under my coat. But as I watched myself, incredulously, almost from outside myself, there I was, shining God's love on that crackhead. Words came through me that were utterly inappropriate for a defenseless man being robbed. In a voice so generous I hardly recognized it as my own, I heard myself say gently, but firmly, "My brother, I used to be an addict too. I bought drugs for years and years and years. I'm not giving any more money to drug dealers."

He looked at me for a moment, bewildered, then softened. "Thank you," he said. All the aggression was gone. The crackhead turned his back to me and walked away.

Time started again. I awoke from the momentary trance, picked up my bags, and hurried toward the hotel, wondering what just happened. On the way home through Atlanta a few days later, I saw on the front page of the paper that the police shot a robber to death in that parking lot. I wondered if it was the same addict, and if it was, whether God sent other angels to try to save His lost sheep from that fatal encounter.

An angel appeared the night Matthew was born. By the time she appeared, Alice had been in hard labor for thirty hours, wracked by Pitocin-induced contractions. In 1998, mothers could not get a spinal anesthetic until their cervix was almost fully dilated and Alice was not yet there, so she endured those thirty hours of labor without any pain relief. She was completely exhausted.

Alice's young obstetrician said that the baby's vital signs were unsteady. The baby seemed to be positioned so that he crimped the umbilical cord. Staring at the fetal monitor, the OB finally shook her head. "I'm going to scrub," she said. "We need to do a C-section."

Alice was on her fourth shift of nurses. As soon as the obstetrician left to scrub for the operation, the new nurse who had arrived with the OB for this visit stepped close and straightened Alice's bedding. The nurse was Chinese, which immediately struck me as a nice coincidence. It wasn't common to see other Chinese people in Princeton then, except on campus. Alice missed her community sometimes. Princeton was pretty white.

The nurse immediately connected with Alice. "Try this," she said, propping Alice up with pillows, gently but firmly adjusting her. "Baby will like this." After the nurse repositioned Alice, she stared intently at the fetal monitor.

A few tense moments passed before her face split open with a grin. "Working!" she said. "I tell the doctor." She turned to Alice and paused before rushing out. "No C-section for you!" she pronounced, beaming at Alice. "You deliver baby!".

The nurse returned with the OB in her operating gown in tow. "See?" the nurse said, stabbing her finger at the monitor. "Baby happy!" The obstetrician stared at the monitor for a minute, then nodded to the nurse and left. The nurse was ecstatic. "No C-section for you! You deliver baby!" She announced again, triumphantly.

An hour later, Alice got her spinal block and was in screaming final contractions. "Baby coming down!" the nurse yelled. Matthew was crowning. We could see his thick black hair, matted with amniotic fluid. Then he stopped progressing through the birth canal. His vitals on the monitor faltered. The obstetrician looked concerned again.

The nurse had been standing next to the OB as the OB tried to guide Matthew out. Now, she came around the side of the bed so that her mouth was right next to Alice's ear. Firmly, lovingly, as if Alice was her own daughter, the Chinese nurse held Alice's hand and prodded her on. As the nurse worked with Alice, it struck me that the nurse sounded *exactly* like Alice's mother.

During the wait for final labor to begin, while Alice was dozing, the nurse asked me about Alice's family's background. It turned out that the nurse grew up in Hong Kong at the same time as Alice's mother and came to the States in the early 1970s as well, after the US eased restrictive Chinese immigration quotas lingering from the 1886 Chinese Exclusion Act. Their common cultural heritage explained why the nurse had the same speech patterns as Alice's mother, with the same impatience for superfluous English articles. The similarity in the way they spoke was eerie. The nurse was virtually channeling Alice's mother, but with a softness that Alice's mom could rarely show after all the hard knocks she overcame as a refugee from Japanese invasion in Hong Kong and as a deserted single mother of three young children in New York.

As the nurse worked with Alice, coaching and encouraging her in Alice's mother's best voice, the OB faded away; it was all Alice and the nurse, with Alice, pressing on beyond the limits of endurance to continue her pushing. Impossibly, with the nurse's inspiration, Alice found a last reservoir of strength and out came Matthew. We were parents.

Another squad of professionals moved purposefully through the post-natal checks and clean-up, and the nurse, Alice's angel for the crucial hours needed to safely usher Matthew into the world, was gone.

Alice collapsed into the deep sleep of physical exhaustion. The staff attending to Matthew proclaimed him healthy. Soon he was clean. Since Alice was unconscious, they handed the swaddled baby to me. Matthew gazed at me, wide-eyed.

Let me digress from angels to reflect on becoming a parent. I was never fond of babies. I don't think I held more than one before Matthew, and that was my first nephew, thirty years earlier. I had no drive to be a parent, but I recognized that Alice did, and parenting was our logical next step after five years of marriage. When they put our child in my arms and he looked up at me, it was like plugging a battery into a circuit I didn't know existed. The parenting circuit lit up and I was instantly, hopelessly, blindly in love. Through misty eyes, I promised Matthew that I would always take care of him, knowing this was impossible but that I had to try. The parental love circuit has been on for twenty years now, lit up just as strongly for Joe and Jane.

There is no perfect metaphor for the incomprehensible divine. As the Bible says, "Now we see things imperfectly, like puzzling reflections in a mirror."[13] I never liked the parent metaphor for God, which I always viewed from the son's side. My earthly father, like all earthly fathers, was rife with human failings, and no one can spot them or feel victimized by them more effectively than an ungrateful, rebellious child. Who wanted a father-god like that?

Now, with Matthew swaddled in my arms, for the first time I understood the metaphor from the parent's perspective. This blind love for my child was a taste of how God loves us so completely, irrespective of our imperfections.

As our next two children arrived, I understood how a parent, and the God who created parenthood, could love all their children just as fully as they loved each one. It wasn't dividing a fixed pie of love from one, into two, then into three, so that each additional child reduced the others' share. For a human parent, there might be limits on time to apportion among their children, but there is a bottomless love for each of them, complete and undiminished by their number.

As the children matured, I also began to understand why God sometimes felt more distant and less obviously interventional in my life as I matured spiritually. That's what good parents do. When our children really need us, it's our job to be right beside them. When they don't really need us (even if they think they still do), it's our job to withdraw a little, and then a little more, to let them take the risks of growing, knowing they will make mistakes and that they will get hurt. Good parenting brings the excruciating anxiety of watching your precious little one wobble along on her bike as you stop running beside her and let her go ahead of you for the first time, or seeing your defenseless little boy get on the school bus for the first time and ride off, or turning away in sudden tears as your beloved child closes the door to his freshman dorm between you.

When I really need God to reveal Himself, like I do now as I prepare to leave everyone I love and swore to protect to His care, He comes close and whispers His reassurances in all the subtle and not so subtle acts of grace that envelop us. It doesn't stop all the pain of impending separation from those I love, but God's presence makes it endurable and leaves the hope, which at its strongest becomes an expectation and occasionally even a certainty, that while God empowered me to provide for the continuity of my family's daily rhythms and relationships after I go home through savings and life insurance, I am only one medium to bring God's grace and God's love to my family. God will love and care for my family after I cross over through other vehicles, other angels. Like the Apostle Paul: "I am convinced that neither death nor life, neither angels nor demons, neither the present nor the future, nor any powers, neither height nor depth, nor anything else in all creation, will be able to separate us from the love of God …" 14

And, while God is calling me home sooner than expected, I can't really know what I will miss as a result of not living into my eighties or nineties. Yes, I will miss seeing my children become adults, but I have lived long enough to know that these kids will turn out well. They are good people, with talent, sharp minds, morality, a taste of God, and a work ethic. They will grieve my passing, as we all grieve our parents' passing, and I am sad when I think that anything involving me will hurt them that way, but I can't know how the story would go if I lived longer. Isn't it possible that they will they be spared a worse tragedy by my going home now? If I lived longer, might I have continued driving like a Pennsyltucky redneck as my perception and reflexes dimmed, so that I ended up I hurting or killing someone – perhaps one of them – in a wreck? Might I have had a long, wasting disease like my mother that strained and drained my family for years? Might my charming inability to remember names and facts have devolved into dementia? Might that weekend just after college spent repainting the sooty acoustic tiles at my ad firm's office, only to find what

I now know to be asbestos tiles stashed above them that I had to move around for two days, have caught up with me? It only takes one fiber and I'd take what I have over asbestosis anytime.

God alone knows how the story would go if I lived longer, but the God who knows that loves me and my family, and I strongly suspect God is ordering my time on this side in this way with mercy and for good reason. As the hymn goes, we may only understand the rationale for God's timing in calling us home, some at four and some at a hundred and four, "bye and bye," when we are reunited with God and later with each other on the other side of the veil.[15]

In the meantime, the comfort is to trust in His love, which we have seen, and to trust that love motivates all of His actions with us.

JACOB AND LABAN

After I discovered that there is a God, I had to learn what God would and wouldn't do, which lessons God would reveal to me and what I would have to discover on my own through trial and error. My default remained self-reliance, so I had to continually "get a bigger God," as they say in AA. I needed a God powerful and involved enough to oversee everything I worried about, and one of my biggest worries was work. Amazingly, God showed up there too.

Being a lawyer was not my lifelong dream. I went to law school after foundering as a commercial artist. I was a talented amateur but lacked the skills and the drive to make it in the big league of commercial art, or even in the minors. After two years of deficit spending at the bottom rung of the New York advertising art world, my savings were exhausted. I branched into sales first, then finance. I sold my car and then the motorcycle that replaced it, then resorted to borrowing to bridge the gap between my income and my living expenses. It was time for a reset.

My roommate in New York was a Colgate classmate attending Fordham Law School. I liked his law school friends and liked several of my other Colgate classmates who had gone on to law school. I couldn't imagine creating my own career path from the chaos of the business world and appreciated that law had a well-defined ladder to climb. A successful legal career started with a standardized test and I was good at standardized tests. LSAT scores determined law schools, law school class rank determined law firm or clerkship offers, and associate output determined partnership. My parents cut me off financially when I graduated college on the sound theory that I should be able to support myself with a four-year degree, but they would raid my grandfather's trust again to pay for graduate school. Not only did law school seem doable for all these reasons, it was a real profession. Being a lawyer would redeem me in the eyes of my family, friends, and potential mates after my washout in the art world. I never gave a minute's thought to whether I would like doing what lawyers do before embarking on my legal career. I didn't go to law school because I wanted to lawyer. I went because I wanted to be a lawyer. I only saw the noun, with all its perks, not the verb, with all its headaches.

I liked law school. It was the first time I applied myself to my studies and, after struggling to make a living for two years, I was highly motived and comparatively disciplined. I was able to cram my drinking into weekends and breaks. I finished *cum laude* and was offered an associate's position at New York's biggest insurance defense firm. The tort boom was underway and they were swamped with business. The firm placed me in the product liability group under one of the founders, a tall, quiet, principled man. He asked me if I would rather defend chemicals or machines. I said machines. I liked working on my car as a teenager. He asked me if I would rather defend tractors or motorcycles. I told him I rode motorcycles. That was it. I was the new associate on a motorcycle account.

The hot new product in the motorcycle industry was three-wheeled all-terrain vehicles, motorized tricycles with oversized low-pressure tires. They were fun to ride, but as with every cycle, a proportion of their riders ended up in hospital emergency rooms. ATV-associated emergency room visits created a new spike that caught the attention of the Consumer Product Safety Commission's injury monitoring system. American society accepted comparable injury levels for motorcycling, snowmobiling, football, bicycling, and skiing, but times had changed since those sports entered the mainstream and society would not tolerate a new sport with a similar risk level. The CPSC began investigating all-terrain vehicles and found them a convenient target. The manufacturers were foreign, with most ATVs made in Japan, which was encountering high trade friction over its rapid penetration of the US auto and appliance markets. ATV riders were neither wealthy nor organized. With few friends in Washington, three-wheeled ATVs were ultimately barred from the US market.

I was assigned to ATVs just as product liability litigation drafting on the CPSC investigation took off. I rode that horse for fifteen years, the first ten at a gallop, spending a third of each year on the road to cover expert and plaintiff depositions, two dozen trials of up to a month each, product and accident scene inspections, mediations, defense expert meetings, and witness preparation sessions in California and Japan. For the first five years, I was still drinking, but was able to find clients who drank hard too and appreciated my generous use of the firm's entertainment budget to cover our bar tabs, so it worked out until it didn't. Then I got sober.

The watershed moment that redefined the second half of my legal career came in 2000. After seventeen years as a litigator, now attending to a growing, multinational manufacturing client I brought in as the ATV litigation waned, twelve years sober in AA, nine years of aspiring to follow Christ, eight years of marriage, and a year and change of parenthood, I hit a wall and had to invite God into my career.

By the fall of 2000, I was completely wrapped around the axle at work. Forty-five and worn out from years of unremitting high-wire litigation, I felt like I just had to suck it up and trudge another twenty years to retirement. Always a little rebellious, I was frustrated with the politics and bureaucracy of big firm life. I was good at navigating it and had rapidly become a partner and then an equity partner with a corner office overlooking midtown Manhattan, but political success at the firm seemed to come at an unacceptable cost to my integrity. The leadership's opaqueness, occasional heavy-handedness, and its perceived inequity struck a Celtic bone that demanded greater independence from management's yoke. There's a reason my ancestors, hill people from Northern England, Scotland, and Northern Ireland, were consigned to the frontier wilds of Appalachia and to Canada's southern border. We like our space and our freedom, and we'll fight to protect it.

So it was that, channeling a Blue Ridge mountain man catching a sheep rustler red-handed, I went off like a bottle rocket at a meeting of all the partners in our practice group after a partner I didn't like announced that a top associate I hired and groomed for my team would be moving to the firm's suburban office to work with him.

There were perhaps thirty male and female partners around the big boardroom table, methodically sorting through the logistics of moving most of our practice group to the suburban office (I would stay in New York) when the partner I didn't like dropped this bomb. All my tightly-wound frustrations unspun. I stared darkly at the offending partner and said, with what I hoped was icy resolve, that the associate had said nothing to me about moving and was essential to my team.

Open confrontation like this was not typical in our group meetings. You had to feign kumbaya or be marked as a troublemaker with no path to firm management. All eyes were on me. The associate-rustling partner, smiling sheepishly, said he talked with the associate and it was all set. That did it. The steam building up in me instantly overpressurized and my boiler blew (an event called a "puff" in the understated vernacular of pressure vessels to describe a phenomenon that can level a building and throw five-hundred-pound debris a football field away). Without a millisecond's consideration, I announced to the group in the coarsest possible terms that I preferred being romanced before my partners made sport with me. I walked out of the meeting, leaving my colleagues in stunned silence.

The barroom blowhard had not been heard from so clearly in twelve years. I was drunk on self-righteous rage. Waiting for the elevator outside the conference room, I dialed my big client's litigation director. When he picked up, I would say, "I'm leaving. Will you come with me?" The elevator arrived before my call rang through, so I hung up and rode to the ground floor. I knew I had to clear the building and cool off. I dialed my client again as I wove through the crowd toward the subway entrance at Grand Central. Again, the call did not go through, so I headed underground. I'd call the litigation director from Brooklyn.

With thirty-five minutes underground, rocking along in the familiar cocoon of a half-empty, off-peak train, reason crept back in and I began to survey the wreckage from my outburst. After a decade of AA, I knew there was no justifying it, no matter how legitimate my frustrations might be. As my AA friend Crying Cathy used to say, "Self-righteous anger is like peeing in your pants. It feels good at first. Then, it's embarrassing." I was over the feeling good part. As soon as I emerged into the sunny, tree-lined streets of Park Slope, I dialed my practice group leader to apologize for my language and behavior. He had been trying to reach me while I was in the subway. He apologized for the way the news was sprung on me and said that management would revisit moving my associate (he stayed).

I had known for a long time that my approach to work was inconsonant with the spiritual path laid out by Christianity and AA. In hindsight, I feel like after my tantrum at the partners' meeting, I was due for a timeout. It came in the form of a cancer diagnosis three months later, which required surgery and then a month off work.

I do not blame God for my cancer. I smoked for twenty years, drank far too much, and used drugs compounded by people who did not have my best interests or FDA good manufacturing practices in mind. I worked with carcinogens as a commercial artist without adequate ventilation. Aside from all the environmental factors, genetics testing suggests that the cancer might have arisen from latent damage caused by crashing my mom and dad's DNA together in utero.

While I don't believe God gave me cancer, I do believe that God used the opportunity created by the forced hiatus cancer gave me from work to clear my head and show me a healthier, spiritually-centered way to approach my job. As the Apostle Paul said: "[W]e know that in all things God works for the good of those who love him, who have been called according to his purpose"[16]. During that unplanned month off work, bathed in the clarifying new awareness that a long, healthy life wasn't guaranteed, I realized that I couldn't wait until retirement, after slogging and battling through a career, to do the things God put me here to do. I had to find a way to live my life fully now, in the middle of the march.

Before I went back to work after the surgery in early 2001, Alice and I met with a financial planner. I did not want to ever again become so obsessed with office politics. There had to be another way. Maybe I should become a law school professor. I didn't like teaching, but surely academia would be less stressful. The financial planner would tell us if we could afford a job change like that.

When we ran the numbers, there was no denying that we had an expensive lifestyle. We lived in Park Slope. We expected Matthew to go to private school. We hoped for more children. While our lifestyle was expensive, we were paying for things of value and not for baubles, so we did not feel that living as we did was necessarily an extravagance that should be reined in to permit another job I might like more. Our lifestyle was only sustainable if I continued to work as a law firm partner.

I didn't hate being a lawyer. I was just stuck in a negative way of doing the job of lawyering. I asked the planner what would happen if I cut back my billable hours to devote more time to the things that fed my soul – my family, my health and my spiritual practices — and eased off on the office politics, with some resulting impact on my career. What if because of those adjustments, my gross pay dropped by, say, thirty percent?

The planner punched a few numbers into a big calculator on his desk and responded: "You would have to work to sixty-seven and have a little less money for retirement, but you would be fine." That was it. I didn't need to change my career. I just needed to adjust and reprioritize and not worry so much about extracting the last nickel from it. We would be fine with the financial output from a more balanced approach to work. I thank God for using the first bout with cancer to show me that.

And here's the thing: when I stopped going to work with gritted teeth, made a little more time for the things that nourished my soul, and loosened up on the office politics outside my control, it showed in my work. I put in less time, enjoyed what I did more, did the job more effectively, and my clients responded with more work, for which I made more money.

Along the way, I saw how I could bring God's love into the rough and tumble world of product liability litigation. First, I redefined my job from fighting adversaries to resolving disputes. Jesus said that peacemakers are blessed and gunslingers get shot.[17] More materially, the compromise value of cases floats as facts helpful to either side come out in discovery. If my ego wasn't tied up in trying to crush the enemy in mortal combat at my clients' expense, I could end the clients' litigation burn as soon as a case's settlement price favored my client. I found that most of the time, after some initial testing and fact-gathering, we could resolve disputes informally through negotiations or a mediation. When we couldn't, we could ask a jury to resolve the dispute formally, through a trial. Either way, the goal was not beating the adversary, the goal was ending the dispute on terms my client could accept.

When we went to trial or argued a motion or an appeal to a judge, my role was no longer to persuade the jury or the judge to go my client's way. My goal was to try to present my client's side of the case in the clearest, most persuasive way I could that day. How the judge or the jury decided the issue was out of my control, and therefore none of my business (although I certainly preferred, as did my clients, when the judge or jury agreed with our position). That little shift from trying to persuade to trying my best to present persuasively took much of the pressure out of trials and oral arguments by redirecting my focus to something I could control – my preparation and my presentation – instead of trying to control things that I could never control – the minds and actions of judges or juries. My litigation outcomes improved when I attended to my part and left the results to God.

The plaintiffs in the lawsuits I defended were often terribly injured, or they were parents of a child who was terribly injured or dead. Their lawsuits usually lacked merit. My Japanese and German clients generally built a reasonably good, if not exceptionally good, product. Plaintiffs' counsel relied on jury sympathy to overcome dispassionate analysis, which it often does. But I no longer blamed the plaintiffs for going to lawyers to try to pursue financial security for themselves or their families in the wake of expensive, disabling injuries and a flawed social net.

By bringing a suit, the plaintiffs were signing on to face a defense lawyer in deposition, which could be very stressful. They would have to relive their accident and treatment in excruciating detail, and their lawyer would probably want them to lie about key points of the accident scenario. If I was the defense lawyer they faced, their interrogator would be courteous and calm. They would usually grant me more concessions than they would grant an attack dog lawyer who made them defensive and helped them rationalize telling lies.

With time, the clients who wanted attack dog litigators with their swaggering promises to crush the plaintiffs in deposition and thrash the plaintiffs' lawyers at trial faded away. I ended up surrounded by more experienced and realistic clients. They wanted a lawyer who would resolve their disputes efficiently without unnecessarily brutalizing their injured customers or wasting money on needless procedural squabbling. Clients like that tended to be grounded, principled, decent people. As seniority and good results brought bigger cases, my opposing counsel were more likely to avoid needless procedural confrontation that would not advance their cause, unlike the lawyers who handled smaller cases and lacked the confidence to be diplomatic. That reduced my clients' litigation costs. My work environment gradually became much more pleasant as my clients and adversaries evolved into the kind of people I enjoyed working with. After I let God shape my work life, it became far less stressful.

In 2007, four other equity partners and I started our own firm, choosing people and a partnership arrangement that made going to the office more collaborative. When I finally left the megafirm seven years after my outburst at the partner meeting and God's subsequent revelation of how to recast my work life during my recovery from my first cancer surgery, my exit from my employer of twenty-four years was neither abrupt nor reactive. Instead, it came after five years of patiently trying to resolve my issues with management only to recognize that they were structural, not personal. The firm's growth was taking it in a direction that would not serve my clients. If I stayed at the firm, my clients might leave. And then, as the need to leave clarified, my departure came only after two years of carefully building, testing, and confirming a business plan and developing a logistical timeline for starting another firm.

Leaving a law firm is tricky business. The way I tried to do it the day of my tantrum seven years earlier was incompetent and illegal. A partner has a fiduciary duty to his partners not to compete with them. He cannot ask firm clients to leave with him, as I would have done if my call to my client had gone through, until he has put his partners on notice that he is departing the firm.

I knew from prior partner departures that the firm played hardball on this. If a departing partner failed to tell the firm he was leaving before he asked the clients for their business as I had tried to do after my tantrum, the partnership would sue him for breaching his fiduciary duties. On the other hand, once a partner told the partnership's management he was leaving, they could hold the departing partner to a ninety-day resignation notice provision of his contract. While he was still bound to the firm as a partner, restrained by his fiduciary duties from competing with the firm for its clients for those three months, the firm could offer those clients alternative services and rate concessions if they stayed instead of leaving with the departing partner. If management got wind that a larger departure like ours involving several partners was brewing, the firm could determine which lawyers were integral to the new firm's launch and offer them big salary increases to stay, leaving the less essential lawyers with a doomed start-up.

Knowing how aggressively the firm would respond if management found out we were plotting a departure, the lawyers planning to depart with me and I had to plan our escape surreptitiously. This meant doing all the logistical work required to start a firm in secret, which did not feel comfortable given that I was trying to live an honest, Godly life.

The final straw that sealed the decision to leave came when the firm, knowing I was frustrated, asked me how much they needed to pay me to stay. I gave them a fair number. The senior partner responsible for my compensation conceded that the number was reasonable and told me the firm would pay it, but management reneged at year-end because other lawyers had lost money on bad business. I would be punked if I stayed with the firm after I gave them a figure they needed to meet to keep me and they refused to meet it. If I was unwilling to leave after that, I had no negotiating leverage going forward. Hoping the firm might reconsider making good on its promise so that I could stay, I protested the shortfall on my raise and was summoned to a meeting with top management.

The night before the big meeting I was worried. I knew that the firm's leaders would ask me if I planned to leave if the firm didn't come through with the raise. I didn't want to lie, but I knew that if I was open about leaving, management would do whatever it could to make it economically impossible for us to leave with our clients and start a new firm.

A year earlier, I started reading Bible stories to Matthew at bedtime when I saw how thirsty he, like all children, was for a mythos to make sense of the universe. I figured that irrespective of whether he ultimately chose to become a

Christian, he should at least know the mythos that underpins Western civilization, not just the recycled Greek mythology then popular in a series of children's books or the mythos George Lucas and others, mostly dystopians, created to slake that thirst. The children's Bible we used started with the Old Testament stories in rough chronological order, giving historical context and offering lessons to be drawn from the stories. I find the often angry, vengeful God of the Christian Bible's Old Testament hard to reconcile with the loving, forgiving God of the New Testament. It always seemed to me that God came to us as Jesus to show us that God was not the tyrant the Bronze Age writers made Him out to be. While respecting the Old Testament stories as literature and the skeleton of the Western worldview, I had largely steered clear of them. Thus, many of the Old Testament stories were new to me when I read them to Matthew.

Imagine how I felt, given all the things on my mind the night before my showdown meeting with management, wrestling with how to ethically handle the questions that would come in a few hours about whether I planned to leave the firm, when I lay down next to Matthew to read him the next story from his children's Bible and encountered, for the first time, the story of Jacob and his uncle Laban in Genesis 29–31 (quoted here from the NIV).

"After Jacob had stayed with Laban for about a month," the story begins, "Laban said to him, 'You shouldn't work for me without pay just because we are relatives. Tell me how much your wages should be.'"

Wasn't that the same question the firm had asked me?

Jacob tells Laban his terms and Laban agrees to meet them. Hadn't the firm agreed to my terms for staying and working with them? As I continued, the parallels were uncanny. I had the feeling that God was unquestionably using the medium of the ancient text to speak to me. I couldn't wait to see what happened next.

As the firm had done with me, Laban reneged on his side of the deal. What should Jacob, and by extension, what should I, do in that situation? I read on: "Jacob outwitted Laban the Aramean, for they set out secretly and never told Laban they were leaving."

I thought then of how even Jesus, while willing to be martyred in the most awful way when the time was right, avoided unnecessary conflicts that would divert Him from his purpose. He veiled His words in parables. He stole away in darkness to avoid a stoning. He told some He saved with miracles not to speak of it.

I thanked God for showing me how to handle the meeting with the firm's management the next day and slept peacefully. Like Jacob, I would set out in secret and not tell management I was leaving.

I managed through good lawyer's sophistry not to lie at the meeting, but also not to divulge my plans to leave the firm. Thanks to what God had shown me by drawing me to the story of Jacob and Laban at just the right moment for it to be meaningful to me, I was able to see that in this instance my lack of candor was necessary diplomacy and not sinful deceit. My meeting passed with my family's and my partners' families' livelihoods intact until we left months later with all the business we had brought to the firm.

When we left, we followed the rules for partner departures assiduously and had a fully functioning law office waiting for us the day we walked away from the old firm. I thanked God countless times for not letting my calls go through to the client seven years earlier now that I realized all the planning and care and discretion required for a successful departure.

When my partners and I simultaneously emailed our resignations to the partnership and thirty minutes later asked the clients to come with us, we had four rainmakers at the airport on the way to meet with our clients before the firm's emissaries could reach their offices a day or two later.

We had office space rented and furnished, with a working phone and computer on each desk and an office manager keeping things humming. We had a website and email accounts waiting to be switched on. We had insurance and a bank account and a line of credit. We had a registered partnership and a partnership agreement. We scheduled a conference call thirty minutes after the client emails went out with all the associates and staff we would ask to come with us, now fair game since the partnership was on notice. Half our clients signed on with the new firm by noon the day we resigned, and almost all the rest committed to us by close of business. There was nothing to fight about, and the firm let us go without running out our notice period.

Contrast that outcome with the complete disaster my first, spontaneous attempt to leave would have wrought seven years earlier. The difference in maturity is stunning. Surely my first round with cancer had a lot to do with that. It took a major upheaval to blast me out my rut at work and set me on a more rewarding path for the second half of my career. God does use bad circumstances for good.

Having cancer before starting the new firm helped in another way. While none of the other partners, all in our late forties or early fifties, had gotten the memo informing us that we were mortal, I had. Money for nonessentials was tight during our start-up period and my partners questioned the necessity, but I pressed hard for good disability and life insurance benefits. Those benefits are providing for my family now.

I do not have existential doubts about the societal value of my career, even though it was not a traditional do-good job. The law firm my partners and I started put dinner on the table for fifty families for over a decade before I left it. Alice and I tithed ten percent of our earnings to charity, which added up over a thirty-year career as a successful lawyer. We paid another forty percent to federal, state and local government to support services that others could not afford to fund. We paid much of the remaining half of our earnings for full-freight tuition, leaving scholarship funds and merit slots at the best public schools for others who could not so readily earn the kind of money that we could. Alice, who surely has more brains, talent, and initiative than me, was freed to use them in a career and in charitable endeavors that more directly benefited society, while assuring that her children had the financial security so sorely lacking in her early life. I have no regrets about my career choice, once God helped me see it as service to Him. It was a rewarding, interesting, and honorable way to make a living.

CANCER ROSHI

While God can work good from whatever besets us, as my friend Angela used to say, "A lot of good gifts come badly wrapped." Our goals get frustrated. We often don't get what we want and we lose what we treasure. We, and everyone we care about, age and get sick and die. The Kingdom of God is around us, right now, right here, but this material realm that we live in, despite the radiant wind of the divine blowing through it, can be hard. Thankfully, God has a way of forming pearls of wisdom, acceptance, love, and faith around the grit that irritates us.[18] Let's talk more, then, about how God used the "emperor of maladies" as my greatest teacher.

2000 – The Guided Missile

In the fall of 2000, amid the mounting frustration with my firm that would soon lead to my infantile explosion at the partners' meeting, flu vaccine was in short supply. The early batches of vaccine were rationed to the most vulnerable populations. The rest of us would have to wait until January 2001 for ours. With an eighteen-month-old in the house, I needed a flu shot and in late November I scheduled an appointment with our GP (this was before pharmacies could dispense vaccines) to get one in January.

A couple of weeks before my flu shot appointment, on a predawn morning in December 2000, Matthew woke early, as he often did. Desperate for another hour of sleep, I took Matt into a room with a futon, a small TV, and a videocassette player. I put a cartoon video that Matthew liked into the VHS player, closed the door to corral him, turned out the lights, hit play, and passed out on the futon.

I was jarred awake by a jolt and searing pain in my right side. While I slumbered, Matthew stacked up a pile of couch pillows, scaled them, and leapt off, landing with his knee focusing all the impact into my right side. It should have hurt, but not like this. After a while, the pain settled down and I fell back asleep for a few more precious minutes.

A couple days later, in a hotel on a business trip, I took a pee and saw blood in the bowl. It scared the daylights out of me. The bleeding continued intermittently over the next several days. I dreaded taking a wiz and seeing the dark fluid leaking out of me.

I played rugby in college and had heard of people getting bruised kidneys. I assumed that Matthew's leap in the dark must have bruised my right kidney – that was why it hurt so much. I assumed that the bruised kidney would bleed a little and then heal. The blood in the bowl was terrifying, but not enough to warrant an unmanly trip to a doctor who would surely just tell me to wait it out so the kidney could heal on its own.

I had that early January appointment scheduled for the flu shot, though. As I buttoned my shirt after the shot, I figured I might as well mention the bruised kidney and let my GP confirm that it was nothing. Dr. Schwartzburt seemed more concerned than I expected. She said that it took a lot more than a bump in the night from a toddler to start a healthy kidney bleeding – more on the lines of a car crash. She urged me to get an ultrasound. That sounded like overkill. She said it might turn out to be nothing, but I was insured and it wouldn't cost me a penny. Why not rule out anything serious?

I had the ultrasound. Then, at the imaging center's recommendation, I had a CT. There was a substantial mass in my right kidney. The radiologist wasn't certain, but it might be cancer. It was surreal. Cancer was something that happened to other people, not to me, at forty-five.

I called my dad the radiologist. He asked for the images and I sent him a DVD. He immediately stepped in as my case manager, assisted by my stepmother, a sharp and efficient former x-ray technologist. Dad worked his network and shopped the images to the best cancer centers in the country – Cleveland Clinic, MD Anderson, Johns Hopkins, Sloan Kettering.

After a couple days, Dad reported back. The consensus was that the mass was cancerous, even though I was young for kidney cancer. After Dad read the reports and studies on kidney cancer treatment, he determined that the best doctor for younger kidney cancer patients was Dr. Paul Russo at Memorial Sloan Kettering Cancer Center in Manhattan. I was happy to hear that it was not someone in Cleveland or Houston or Baltimore. I could walk to Sloan Kettering from my house if I didn't want to spend $2.25 for the forty-minute subway ride.

As it turned out, of all the oncologists in all the cancer centers in all the world, my dad knew Dr. Russo. Dr. Russo's father was a doctor in Ithaca, New York, not far from where we grew up in northcentral Pennsylvania. Dr Russo's father had arranged a college internship for Dr. Russo at my dad's hospital twenty-five years earlier. I also learned that Dr. Russo graduated two years ahead of me from Colgate. Thankfully, he applied himself much more diligently to his studies, but we still had an immediate affinity that was reassuring.

Stop here for a second. What are the odds that the best doctor in the country for my condition would be found seven miles from my house, and that as I sat in front of his desk for my initial consultation, my father knew him and we went to college together? Scared as I was at having kidney cancer, I had the feeling God was drawing close, bending the probabilities to let me know that He was moving around me to make this easier.

I was unprepared for the emotions attending my first brush with mortality. Before I saw Dr. Russo, I made the mistake of researching kidney cancer on the internet. What I learned was not reassuring. The odds of someone my age getting kidney cancer were sixty thousand to one. The odds of someone diagnosed with kidney cancer surviving five years were then on the order of sixty percent. While that was a majority, I didn't find the statistic reassuring. If one arrow fired in the air could find me in a small city of sixty thousand, how safe was I from four arrows pointed at a group of ten?

It was unbearable to think that an early death might separate me from my child. I could not look at Matthew without falling apart.

Dr. Russo offered some reassurance. The problem with kidney cancer, he told me, was that it often doesn't throw off obvious symptoms until it has spread to other organs. I had a dull back ache for months before my diagnosis, but what forty-five-year-old with a small child, twenty extra pounds, and a desk job didn't? I had been admitted to the ER several times over the prior year for unexplained bouts of high fever, but we assumed that was just exhaustion from working hard, commuting, and caring for an infant. None of the treaters suspected cancer. If it had not been for Matthew's unprecedented leap into my kidney that night, setting off the blood in my urine, the kidney cancer might well have gone undetected until it was too widespread to treat. Because my cancer was caught before it metastasized and became more symptomatic, instead of the normal sixty percent, Dr. Russo said my five-year survival odds were more like ninety-five percent. Matthew, it seems, had been a guided missile, his actions directed by God so that my cancer would be discovered and treated before it had spread beyond my kidney.

Moreover, if I had not had an appointment with Dr. Schwartzburt scheduled shortly after Matthew banged into my kidney, the bleeding his impact initiated might have subsided without leading me to any follow-up examination. If I hadn't seen a doctor shortly after the bleeding happened, the cancer would have escaped the kidney and put me in a much more precarious position. I didn't have any other doctors' appointments scheduled after the flu shot. If Matthew had made his leap two weeks after my flu shot instead of two weeks before, the bleeding that followed might not have been enough to get me to a doctor. No, too many independent circumstances had aligned for me to imagine that my early diagnosis and my subsequent direction to Dr. Russo were accidental.

With hindsight, I've learned that God always prepares me for what's coming. Years before my cancer scare, I had been inspired – which felt more like being driven by unseen forces – to rise early every morning for many months researching and writing a New Testament-based understanding of unjust suffering, or why terrible things happen to innocent people. It gave me a conceptual framework for reconciling my cancer diagnosis with a loving God.

At the end of that study, I concluded that while God is not the source of death and war and disease in New Testament theology,[19] there is no denying that God, if He is truly omnipotent, has the power to prevent or reverse it. Bewilderingly, sometimes God spared people from calamities in the most dramatic ways – healing the blind and the lame and even restoring the dead to life - but most times God seemed not to intercede. God loves us, the New Testament is crystal clear about that, but God will not necessarily spare us.

While God often allows our suffering, I was struck in my study by the shortest and, to me, one of the most telling verses in the Bible: "Jesus wept."[20] Jesus, better than any of us, knew that our human existence is ephemeral. He, better than any of us, was assured that there is a perfect life of the spirit awaiting us. In the setting of the verse, Jesus even knew that God would soon work through Jesus to undo the death of Jesus' friend Lazarus, which occasioned the grief among Lazarus' survivors that welled up in Jesus' heart until He wept. That verse told me that God, while sometimes allowing severe hardship to beset us, understands through His mortal incarnation as Jesus how agonizing these experiences can be for us, and in His love, God empathizes with us. More poetically, He weeps with us (more about the lessons on grieving I draw from this story later). But, empathize as the Christian God does, there is no doubt that He still often lets painful things happen.

I ultimately concluded that God lets these painful things happen because God must, for reasons I cannot expect to fully understand. Perhaps God allows them most of the time so that we can have the comfort of a dependable world. Perhaps God allows it so we do not mistake our temporal world for our real home in the spiritual dimension. Perhaps God allows it because it is through deep realization of our frailty and inadequacy that we turn to God, the only source of true peace. I have come to believe that the unfairness of much of life's suffering can only be reconciled with a loving, omnipotent God if we are willing to consider a life of the soul that extends beyond the mortal plane. In some cases, it seems, the books only get balanced on the other side, in that place where my mother's years of unspeakable agony could yield endless grace and love and quiet joy.

My study of the New Testament's teachings on unjustified suffering began as I watched a couple my age go through the horror of seeing their beautiful, innocent, recklessly loving four-year-old boy descend overnight from fine health into a series of wasting medical crises that tortured him to death over a year. Understandably, it drove his parents half-mad. The father raged against fate. He did not want to hear anything about a loving God who would let this happen to his child. I don't blame him. I don't know how I would have borne what they bore. One time I tried to say something consoling. "I can imagine how you must feel," I told the boy's father. He turned and stared at me, enraged. "You have no idea how I feel," he spat, and walked away. He was right. How could I? I didn't even have children yet. I hadn't experienced a parent's love, much less the agony of seeing a child die, slowly and awfully.

Months later, after I was inspired by his ordeal to pour hundreds of hours into the theological search for a New Testament Christian response to unjust suffering, I found myself sitting across the aisle from the boy's father, Jim, on the train ride home to Princeton. We started talking and learned that we had common history. Twenty years earlier we had both motored from our upstate colleges in British Leyland two-seaters, my Triumph TR-4A and his Austin Healey, on what were undoubtedly some of the same nights, to chase Skidmore coeds in the same Saratoga bar. Now, we had given up drinking and were commuting together from Princeton to New York. Somehow, we segued from that into a discussion of my writing on unjust suffering. When we got off the train, Jim asked to see it. "Oh," I said to God driving home from the station, "that's why you had me write this." Jim and I grew close after that and he entrusted me with some of the hardest memories of his ordeal.

Jim was still pissed at the idea of God two years later when I emailed him about my diagnosis. "Where's your loving God now?" he replied. The work God called me to do years earlier informed my answer. "Right here," I responded honestly, evident in the unlikely chain of events that led to my early diagnosis and my treating with Dr. Russo in my backyard: "God is right here." Yes, a loving God let me get cancer, but when I really needed God, God drew close and made His presence known to me through these impossibly improbable non-coincidences.

Dad became an earthly angel when I really needed him to, hovering over me throughout that first round with cancer, then leaving as soon as I was cleared after the operation with a good post-surgical prognosis. It was another affirmation of how God "the father" acts, retreating as I matured like a good parent to let me test and strengthen my faith and my character, but swooping back in like my earthly father had when I truly needed His direct intervention again.

Dr. Russo usually had a months-long waiting list, but he repaid my father's kindness to him in granting that college internship by getting me into surgery quickly when a patient cancelled. Thus, it was only for a couple of weeks that I had to endure the fear of my potential separation from my family from a surgical complication or a surgical finding that the cancer was more widespread than the x-rays revealed.

I continue to be amazed now at how freely God moves backward and forward through time; how, knowing that Dr. Russo would become the doctor to treat the cancer I would get in 2000, God could use my father's love for me to engineer that internship for Dr. Russo in the 1970s. Dad didn't know at the time that granting that internship was an act of love for me, but it turned out to be. God knew it would become an act of parental love, and God gave Dad and me that gift. I had the same sense of dad caring for me years later as I slid through a CT donut that would help the doctors track and treat my cancer. My dad devoted his professional life to the nascent field of conventional tomography, the predecessor to computerized tomography. I could feel how Dad's love for tomography was actually love for me, now that tomography was prolonging my life decades later. God created Dad's professional passion and then transfigured it into a father's palpable love for his son. God's love is sublime like that.

The surgery was successful. It confirmed that the miraculous early diagnosis flowing from Matthew's guided missile strike caught the tumor before it escaped into my lymph nodes. Dr. Russo removed half of my right kidney, leaving good margins around the tumor. The standard protocol back then was to remove the entire kidney. These partial nephrectomies were Dr. Russo's contribution to the science for younger patients who could not survive many years of dialysis if they had the entire diseased kidney removed, then lost the other. I still had one and a half kidneys, plenty to do their job of filtering waste, toxins and excess water from my blood. Even if a bilateral tumor developed in my left kidney and necessitated its removal, I could probably still run on what was left of my right kidney without dialysis.

The postoperative pain from the fourteen-inch incision in my side was exquisite. I was on an intravenous morphine pump in the hospital and then released home, still in paralyzing agony with every cough and shift using the severed muscles, armed with a bottle of Percocet, a powerful narcotic pain reliever. This was not a good situation for a recovering addict, but God had given me the information I needed to negotiate it. A night or two before the surgery, I mentioned the pain relievers I would be given at an AA meeting. A woman who had undergone major surgery came over after the meeting and said, simply, "Remember that painkillers are for physical pain." Someone else said, "They are to be taken as needed, not as wanted." After a few days at home, as I reached for the Percocet bottle, it struck me that my pain was now endurable and I was really reaching for the bottle to lighten my mood. I was already in the addictive cycle of emotional peaks and valleys. From experience, I knew it would only get harder to quit if I continued deeper into that cycle, so I stopped taking the Percocet and rode through the mild depression of early opiate withdrawal in a day.

As my head cleared, God's grace transformed this frightening first encounter with carcinoma into what the Buddhists call "Cancer Roshi." What Cancer Roshi taught me made my life immeasurably richer for the eighteen years that have followed.

For starters, Cancer Roshi taught me that having a loving God did not mean that I was assured a long and healthy life, but the uncertainty of my future didn't mean God was unfair, or that I needed to feel victimized. God prepared me with the information to avoid feeling victimized by Him at an AA meeting years before.

Wrestling with the diagnosis before I had surgery, I had fallen into the victimization trap, lamenting, "Why me?" Immediately, the words shot back: "Why not me?" Some people get kidney cancer in their forties. Why shouldn't I be one of them? Because I was smart, or a professional, or from a privileged background? Steve Jobs died young of cancer and he co-founded Apple. Should I be spared because I was sober? Dr. Bob Marshall, AA's co-founder, died of colon cancer.

I remembered then where I had first heard the words, "Why not me?" I was newly sober and listening to a speaker with AIDS at a midtown AA meeting. There was no treatment for AIDS in 1988. The speaker was going to die a hard death from it, but he was happy. He said that he too had asked God, "Why me?" Inspired, he answered himself: "Why not me? I did the things that people do to get AIDS.

Why shouldn't I get it?" Then came the amazing part. He wasn't angry with God for letting him get AIDS. He was grateful, he said, that God loved him so much that when he went through the stage of his disease's progression where his skin became covered with sores, God blinded him so he wouldn't have to see it. Then, when the sores subsided, God restored his sight. That junkie with AIDS made a powerful impression. It's twenty-nine years later and I remember his talk like yesterday. The man wasn't crazy and he wasn't kidding. He was dying of AIDS and he was happy that God loved him and cared for him. Seeing God's love in the shadows the way that junkie had made the road so much easier than blaming God for the "injustice" of my human experience.

After my surgery, dark thoughts that the cancer would return and plummet me back into anxiety and pain regularly intruded. Worrying about a recurrence stole the joy from the beautiful moments Matthew's guided missile had granted me. The next lesson Cancer Roshi taught me was how to live without worrying that the cancer would return.

Dr. Russo recognized my fears of a recurrence in a cynical comment I made during an early follow-up visit, when we were still holding our breath to see if there was another tumor growing somewhere, perhaps in the other kidney. He noticed that I was gaining weight without the inefficient combustion of a tumor to expend extra calories.

"I don't want to save you from cancer to have you die of a heart attack," he quipped as he listened to my breath with his stethoscope.

"You keep me alive for five years," I responded, "and I'll worry about my weight. I don't want to pass up a good plate of ribs, then die of cancer anyway."

He stopped and eyed me sadly. He had seen this before. "Bob," he said, looking me full in the face, "don't spend your life waiting for the other shoe to drop."

Another way that concept was given to me proved to be a reliable mantra whenever I began dreading a recurrence. "Stick with the diagnosis you've got until they give you another one," I would tell myself. If, at the end of a follow-up examination, Sloan Kettering proclaimed me cancer-free, then I was cancer-free until the next examination. If they diagnosed me with cancer again at the next examination, I would deal with it. Until a qualified doctor diagnosed me with cancer, I was cancer-free, period. Every time I recognized the worries creeping back in, I pulled out my mantra. Had Sloan Kettering diagnosed me with a new cancer? No. Then my current diagnosis is that I am cancer-free. I'll stick with that diagnosis until the doctors give me another. After a while, it became so reflexive I rarely worried about a recurrence.

2008 – Ugandans in the Parlor

Eight years later, in the fall of 2008, after years of cancer-free follow-up exams, I had a new law firm and two more children when a cloud appeared at my annual follow-up. "There's a shadow on the ultrasound of the remaining right kidney," Dr. Russo said. "It's bigger than last year. We need more imaging." No diagnosis yet, so I was still cancer-free, but it was a legitimate cause for concern.

A contrast CT and MRI were inconclusive. The mass in my kidney was looking more like a malignant tumor, but the blood supply to the tumor did not light up clearly enough in the contrast imaging for Dr. Russo to be certain. It could still be benign. Even the mortifying return of blood in my urine didn't nail the diagnosis.

I really wanted that tumor to be benign. I wasn't worried about losing the rest of the right kidney. My left kidney, eight years after my original diagnosis, still showed no signs of a bilateral tumor. I could run fine on it if they removed the remainder of the right one. I was terrified of the surgical pain. One of the worst moments of my life was waking up in the intensive care recovery unit after my first cancer surgery, still groggy from sedation, to find that I couldn't move, I couldn't swallow, and my side hurt more – by a factor of a hundred – than any pain I had ever experienced. The terror of not being able to swallow was alleviated after a very long minute or two when a nurse saw my eyes open and spritzed my mouth, dried out from intubation and mouth breathing, so my tongue unstuck and I could swallow again; but the pain from the fourteen-inch surgical incision in my side was unrelenting for days, relieved only by narcotic induced unconsciousness. I did not want to ever endure that kind of pain again. I asked Dr. Russo if he could do the next surgery laparoscopically, without the big incision. "Laparoscopy," he said, "is another word for 'easy.' This surgery is not easy." To remove the remainder of the right kidney, he would have to work around all the scar tissue on my kidney from the first surgery. There would be a repeat of the first fourteen-inch incision, but this time on my belly, where Dr. Russo would enter to steer clear of the scarring from the earlier right-side incision.

I prayed for the tumor to be benign so Dr. Russo wouldn't have to operate again. And I prayed. And I prayed some more. My whole church began to pray. The congregation of our church was, like most urban American Baptist churches, predominately black. Our part of Brooklyn neighbors a large West Indian enclave. The beating heart of our church was a core group of strong, deeply committed women. You could feel the powerful faith of those wonderful Caribbean ladies reflected in their prayers, and, amazingly, it seemed like the prayers were working! On my next visit with Dr. Russo, he told us that in the latest imaging the tumor looked more like it might be benign. Sloan scheduled me for more scans in three months.

Was it possible prayers really could change the course of my disease? "Keep praying!" I told the church ladies, and on we prayed.

On the next visit, Dr. Russo broke the news that the tumor was now looking more like a malignancy. He thought the mass should come out. I couldn't accept that the prayers weren't working. "Can you do a biopsy to be sure?" I asked. Maybe that would prove definitively that the tumor was benign and I wouldn't need the surgery. Dr. Russo said Sloan Kettering normally didn't do biopsies in this situation because of the risk that when they extracted the biopsy needle it would seed the needle track with cancer cells. Seeing how much I wanted certainty, however, Dr. Russo acceded to my request and scheduled a biopsy.

The biopsy confirmed that I had cancer again. I was crushed. What about my prayers?

As I left Dr. Russo's office with this deflating news, it struck me that the worst part of the surgical experience the first time around, worse even than the physical pain of the surgery itself, was the emotional pain of thinking that I might die and be separated from my child. If that thought took root again, it could loom over every encounter with the family, and this time there were two more children I loved with the same all-encompassing love I had for Matthew when I was having my first round with cancer.

That lingering feeling of sadness over potential separation from the children and Alice was familiar. In other forms, it had been all over my first Fourth Step personal inventory in AA. My first sponsor, Chuck, put a name on it when I read my inventory to him: self-pity. So, my first prayer before I left Dr. Russo's office was to ask God to take my self-pity.

When I got to Brooklyn forty-five minutes later, I came through our front door into an encampment of Africans on the parlor floor, lolling on cots and a foldout couch, dozing through jet lag. The Africans were in New York for fifteen-year-old Nina to have her heart repaired. Nina had a heart defect from birth that would have been repaired in infancy in the US. Since treatment for her heart defect was not available in Uganda, she had grown up with poor circulation. Her scalp was blue from lack of oxygenated blood and she was easily fatigued. A Christian charity arranged for Nina's surgery, and, through our church, the charity coordinated with us to house Nina, her mom, and a Kenyan nurse for several weeks of pre-op and recovery.

As I stepped through the doorway to see Nina smiling weakly at me, it struck me how much better my situation was than Nina's. I was going to have a low-risk surgery at a fabulous hospital a few miles from my home in one of the nicest neighborhoods of a prosperous Western city. The New York City Department of Finance charged us a mansion tax when we bought our townhouse, so I guess it's fair to say we lived in a mansion.

Nina, by contrast, was a fifteen-year-old halfway around the world from her home in a completely alien environment. Just yesterday, we had seen her mother and her take their first wide-eyed step onto the wonder of an escalator. Doctors at a hospital a notch down from Sloan Kettering, from another land and culture, who looked and sounded nothing like Nina, planned to saw open her rib cage, remove her heart, try to keep her body and her heart running on machines while they repaired the defect, then reinstall her heart and take her off the circulation machine. If she was still alive after all that, they would close her ribcage, suture her wounds, and hope, as Nina labored through days in the ICU, that her body would tolerate these insults. If Nina recovered, after a few weeks she would return to a country where, the Kenyan nurse told us over dinner one night, mothers pierce their newborns' ears so their babies are no longer considered perfect to deter kidnappers from stealing the infants from the maternity ward to sacrifice for the success of new commercial towers.

Compared to Nina, I was going in for a manicure, and when our respective procedures were completed, I would return to my magical life in Oz while Nina returned to the poverty and violence of Uganda. My troubles were nothing compared to hers. Try as I might, I simply couldn't feel sorry for myself with Nina in the house. God, who can solve so many disparate problems at once, was not only giving Nina the extraordinary opportunity to have her lifelong ailment healed, He was simultaneously letting Nina's presence answer my prayer to be spared from self-pity.

Again, God was moving freely through time. Alice and I didn't know that I would be having another cancer surgery when we volunteered months earlier to house the Ugandans. If we had known that my cancer would recur, we might well have said no. The Sunday the charity asked our church for volunteers to house the African contingent, we looked around at the other congregants and recognized that we were the only ones with a big townhouse and an empty mother-in-law suite in what had once been a first-floor apartment, with its own kitchen and bath, separated by privacy doors from the rest of the house. We knew that the house was God's, not ours, just as everything else we had was God's, not ours. We were only stewards. If we weren't good stewards with the things God entrusted to us, God would find people who were. God has work to do and needs some level of efficiency from the people who serve as his hands and his feet in this realm. Reluctantly, we said yes.

What about the prayers for healing, though? Why had they seemed to be working, then gone cold? I turned on myself. This cancer was my fault. My lack of faith in the power of prayer caused it. I thought about the Apostle Peter when Jesus, walking across the water toward the boat Peter was on, beckoned him to step from the safety of the boat and walk out on the water to meet Him. Peter took the first steps out of the boat and onto the water on faith, but then he began to question whether God would really allow him to do this. Peter grew fearful and started to sink. Jesus, disappointed in his lack of faith, reached out to catch Peter, admonishing him, "You of little faith, why did you doubt?"[21] Was God now saying that to me?

Mired in that self-flagellating state, I sat in our bedroom and leafed through my Bible, looking for direction and solace. I landed on a scripture or two that had no significance for my situation. Then, my finger stopped at the twelfth chapter of Second Corinthians. These words from the Apostle Paul jumped out at me:

> Therefore, in order to keep me from becoming conceited, I was given a thorn in my flesh, a messenger of Satan, to torment me. Three times I pleaded with the Lord to take it away from me. But he said to me, "My grace is sufficient for you, for my power is made perfect in weakness."

I was transfixed. Like Paul, I too had a thorn in my flesh, in the form of a malignant tumor. Like Paul, I too had pleaded with the Lord to take it away from me. As with Paul, God's answer to me was, "No." Now I knew why God had not healed me. It wasn't my lack of faith. Through the scripture, God was telling me, as He had told Paul: "You do not need me to remove this thorn. I will see you through this challenge and you will see my power working where yours has failed."

A flood of self-reproach drained out of me. I wasn't unfaithful Peter here, I was Paul. God, despite Paul's incredible faith – a faith God used to shape much of Christian theology – refused to grant Paul's multiple entreaties to remove the thorn from his flesh. Was I supposed to have more faith than Paul, who was struck blind on the road to Damascus, persecuted, shipwrecked, flogged, imprisoned, and martyred for his faith? Of course not. Yet notwithstanding Paul's unimpeachable faith, God declined his prayer to be healed. Instead, God made clear that Paul's suffering was necessary, but God would carry him through it. God's grace would be sufficient, He told Paul, and God's power would be perfected despite – even because of – Paul's weakness. There could be no confusion that the monumental works which followed Paul's ungranted prayers for healing were the acts of an omnipotent God, not those of fragile, mortal Paul. God would direct where and how the healing rain of his grace would fall, not Paul, and not me.

The surgery went fine and the pain was bad but not as overwhelming the second time around. Maybe it was knowing it would subside in a few days, while the first time I didn't know how long I would have to endure it. Maybe it was advances in painkillers from Percocet to Oxycodone (and again the day would come, now faster with the Oxy, when I would realize I was reaching for the pill bottle to ward off the sad backwash of chemical euphoria, not for physical pain, and again I had to quit the pills immediately, before it got harder.)

I thought I had learned all Cancer Roshi needed to teach me during my first round with kidney cancer in 2001. I had learned that the future is uncertain, our time here is precious, and all of it must be directed to God's purposes. I learned that the inevitability of mortality and the vagueness of when death will arrive can inspire the present without necessarily freighting it with foreboding.

Those were big lessons, but I also learned something momentous from round two in 2008 and 2009. I learned that, for reasons not mine to know, God may not answer prayers for healing, but God will make His presence known to me when I really need Him to – as he did by putting Nina in our house to answer my prayer to be freed from self-pity and by directing me to Paul's story when I needed to stop blaming inadequate faith for my cancer recurrence. Critically, I learned, as God told Paul, that God's grace is sufficient for me; and, by extension, God's grace will be sufficient for my loved ones through whatever comes. That takes a lot of weight off my shoulders.

2017 – A Curious Fall

Another eight years passed after my second cancer round with no sign of a recurrence. They were great years. The children grew and flowered. The law firm we started prospered. Alice's and my relationship grew stronger and deeper. I took up backpacking and began inching my way toward Maine along the Appalachian Trail.

God began to clear the decks for my third and final round with kidney cancer over a year before it began. Winding up my professional commitments before the new diagnosis was another of Angela's "badly wrapped gifts."

In early 2017, I finished a massive case that had been my primary professional obligation for the preceding two years. After the big case concluded, I had hardly any billable work. My partners noticed the falloff in my billable hours and neither they nor I were happy about it, but I assumed it was cyclical and I would be hitting on all eights again soon enough. For thirty-four years there had always been work. I might as well enjoy the extra family time while I could, I thought. Surely another big case would arrive in due course.

I was a good marketer. I had brought in a quarter of the firm's business and its two biggest cases over the past several years. I was confident I could do it again, but a round of client visits did not yield the next big case, only a smallish commercial case that kept me peddling until June 2017, when it too settled.

Without billable work, I tried to use my professional time productively by catching up on administrative tasks. I worked through closing our unprofitable California office and finding new lawyers for the cases there. I worked with a marketing consultant to arrive at a growth strategy in a down market and rolled it out to the firm. I quarterbacked a website and graphics upgrade to support a tenth-year anniversary rebranding and pushed through the long-delayed completion of a name change that, while politically challenging, was necessary to assure the continued stability of the firm.

Coming into the summer of 2017, with the administrative heavy lifting nearing conclusion and, for the first time in my career, no big new case on the horizon to keep me busy, I wondered what I would do. My billable hours were dismal. My team was occupied with smaller cases, but we were overstaffed by one, and that one was me. I began to think that I would need to begin a phased three- or five-year retirement glide path as contemplated by our partnership agreement. The firm was too small and the market was too tight to carry an unproductive partner taking a full share of the profits. I told my partners that I thought my best use to the firm was as a marketer and account manager, but if I couldn't do that, I would look for service work on the other partners' cases in September 2017, after our August vacation. I didn't want to do that, and wouldn't do it nearly as well or as efficiently as some other partners could, but I had to do something to earn my keep if the next big case didn't come in.

In May 2017, I got a clean bill of health from Sloan Kettering on my annual check-up. In early June, I took advantage of the light work schedule to take a challenging hut-to-hut hike with Matthew on the Appalachian Trail in New Hampshire's White Mountains. The terrain was more difficult than anything I had hiked before. One day, we hiked through a cold, all-day rain that drove some dedicated section hikers we dined with in the hut that night to give up the remainder of their hike, and the next day Matthew led us on a nine-mile leg at a mile an hour up and down two 5,000-foot mountains, with one mile-long stretch effectively climbing hand-over-hand through a running stream. I was relieved and proud to find that I could still complete such a difficult hike at sixty-two years old without falling once.

Then, in July 2017, a month after negotiating forty miles of steep, wet, rocky trail without falling, sometimes exhausted and always with my center of gravity raised by a fifteen-pound day pack, I slipped in my backyard and broke three ribs.

We had been having trouble with our backyard storm drain. Later, we would figure out that two wood planters I built fifteen years earlier had rotted out, allowing dirt to erode into the drain and clog it when it rained. Two weeks earlier, the drain backed up and we had to call in a plumber with a heavy-duty snake to clear it. Now, there was a July downpour and I looked out the back window to see the backyard flooding. If I couldn't clear the drain, a doorwell outside the basement door would fill and then the basement apartment would flood. I grabbed my hand drill and snake attachment, a rain slicker, and the first boots I could find, a pair of huge snow boots. Jane came with me to hold an umbrella over the electric drill, and out into the torrent we went.

It was chaotic. The rain hammered the umbrella so hard Jane and I had to yell to hear each other. I crouched down in the pond that was growing in our backyard and tried unsuccessfully to snake the yard drain. The clog was further down the drainpipe than my snake could reach. I looked at the well by the backdoor. It had a foot of water in it already – halfway up to the transom of the door – and the downspout from the roof was pouring water into it from a joint above the well. That meant that the clog was somewhere past the doorwell drain, so now both the roof and the backyard were draining into the well. The water rose quickly.

I shouted to Jane that we had to move from the backyard drain to the doorwell drain. Maybe we could reach the clog from there and snake it clear. I pulled the snake out of the yard drain, and, trying to keep the electric drill dry under Jane's umbrella, rushed toward the doorwell. Watching the water rising, I missed the second stone step into the doorwell and my clunky snow boots slid out from under me. Holding the drill up to keep from soaking it in the well, I didn't protect myself on the fall and took the impact with the stone ledge on my bottom left ribs. Making a damage check before I got up, I recognized that the ribs hurt like hell and might be broken.

The more immediate problem was the rising water in the doorwell. I still couldn't reach the clog from the doorwell drain with my snake, and we couldn't bail into our neighbor's properly draining yard fast enough. Soon the water lapped over the basement door transom, flooding inside.

The storm passed and Alice called the plumber while Joe and Jane helped the tenants mop the water out of their apartment. With the situation stabilized, I headed to a neighborhood urgent care to get the ribs x-rayed. The doctor at the urgent care did not see a fracture on the x-ray and diagnosed me with bruised ribs. I thought the ribs hurt too much not to be fractured, but by the next day I could move a little more freely.

At Alice's suggestion, I treated with an acupuncturist after my second cancer surgery and the incision seemed to heal faster than after the first surgery. On Saturday, the day after my fall, I decided to see if acupuncture could speed my ribs' healing. My acupuncturist, Dr. Tsang, did not have weekend hours, so I called as soon as I got to my desk on Monday and was able to get an appointment that afternoon.

Dr. Tsang is an internist as well as an acupuncturist. After examining me, he said he could treat my ribs with acupuncture but first I would need an x-ray to ensure that there was no internal bleeding. I told Dr. Tsang that I had been x-rayed at urgent care three days earlier. He responded that sometimes fractures or bleeding don't appear immediately, and I should get another x-ray to be safe. He referred me to a radiology practice several blocks away on Canal Street in Chinatown. I should get an x-ray there and return to his office.

The imaging center was a factory, spread over several floors. The staff and almost all the patients were Asian. With great efficiency, they collected my insurance information and, having cleared payment, sent me back for a chest x-ray.

The intake and x-ray went quickly, but I waited forever for the x-ray to be read and reported. I checked a couple times with the desk, concerned that I might have missed something with the language barrier, but the clerk assured me I would be called as soon as the x-ray report came back.

Then my phone rang. It was Dr. Tsang. "The ribs are fractured," he said, "and there is a shadow behind the ribs that we can't identify from the x-ray. It could just be swelling, but we can't rule out that it's blood. You should get a CT."

Oh boy, I thought. This x-ray factory is trying to sell an expensive CT just for fractured ribs. I protested to Dr. Tsang. "Doctor, with all the x-rays I've had for my kidney cancer, I've had a lot of radiation. I hate to add the radiation from another CT just for broken ribs."

"I think it's indicated," Dr. Tsang replied, and something in the tone of his voice convinced me. I assented and an hour later, after they had cleared the CT with insurance and completed it, I was back in the waiting room. Again, it seemed to take forever for the imaging report to come through. Again, my phone rang. Again, it was Dr. Tsang. "I spoke to the radiologist," he said. "You should come to my office when you get the report." I looked at my watch – it was after five; his office was closed. A shadow of foreboding passed over, but I was not prepared for what I saw ten minutes later when the staff handed me the narrative report and DVD of the images.

I had three or possibly four rib fractures, which only confirmed what I felt and was no big deal. I'd had broken ribs before. They hurt for a while and eventually heal. The report went on to say that the radiologist also saw masses in my lymph nodes and liver suspicious for cancer. I stared at the report for a moment and digested it on the walk to Dr. Tsang's office.

The office was empty when I arrived, except for Dr. Tsang. He looked sad. I jumped in so that he would know he didn't have to break the news to me. "I read the report." I said. "I see that they found masses suspicious for cancer." I assured Dr. Tsang that I would report the findings to Sloan Kettering. He said that after Sloan Kettering weighed in, he could do some acupuncture treatment to help the ribs heal.

I knew cancer in the liver was dire. Sitting in bed with Alice that night, I told her that if this had to come, it was coming at a fortunate time. The kids were older and it was clear they were great people. My career was far enough along that the family should be OK financially on my life insurance. My work seemed to have dried up anyway. I was thirteen years older than Alice, so we could not have expected a long retirement in good health together.

"Do you want to go straight to hospice," Alice inquired dryly, "or should you check in with Sloan Kettering first?" Hmmm. Perhaps I was getting ahead of myself. I remembered my longstanding maxim to stick with the diagnosis I had until they gave me another. The current diagnosis was suspicion of cancer, not cancer. I would deal with a new diagnosis when Sloan Kettering gave me one.

While I had agonized throughout the first seven months of 2017 over my growing failure to pull my full weight professionally, I realize now how important it was to be granted this downtime to watch Joe and Jane growing with their travel baseball teams and to see Matthew naturally assume leadership when my spirits flagged on the New

Hampshire trail. More immediately, without the distraction of a major litigation commitment, I could give the diagnosis my full attention.

Over the next ten days of waiting for a contrast CT at Sloan Kettering and then for the results, I tried to leaven the initial Chinatown CT findings with reasons for hope. I had gotten a clean bill of health from Sloan Kettering six weeks ago. I had no symptoms. I had just hiked that arduous White Mountain section of the Appalachian Trail. Maybe this was just low-quality imaging or over-diagnosing by the Chinatown x-ray factory try to sell me a contrast CT after the regular CT. Besides, hadn't I read somewhere that Lyme disease could create x-ray shadows that look like cancer? Most of my backpacking was in ground zero for Lyme disease exposure. I expected that I would get Lyme disease eventually. It isn't always apparent that you are infected until it spreads. Maybe this was my first indication of longstanding Lyme disease. If so, it was probably treatable with heavy antibiotics. Even if it was cancer, I might get my chemo or radiation merit badge, but Sloan Kettering always had some trick up its sleeve to cure me. The cure would just be more involved this time.

Sloan Kettering's radiology report appeared on the patient web portal where I could access it. The report confirmed that the masses in my lymph nodes and liver were consistent with cancer. Sloan scheduled me to see a new doctor, Dr. Voss, a medical oncologist, a few days before a long-scheduled family vacation in Iceland. In the meantime, Dr. Voss arranged a biopsy so that when we met he would know what type of cancer I had.

Alice and I debated whether we should cancel the Iceland trip. We decided that we wouldn't have the information to make that decision until we saw Dr. Voss, just five days before departure.

Then, I got the first of many "God bumps" (an AA term for non-coincidences) to reassure me of God's presence and care as I entered this new and frightening walk into Psalm 23's "valley of the shadow of death." One morning during the anxious interval after the Sloan x-ray report confirmed the metastatic cancer but before we saw Dr. Voss to find out if we could still take the Iceland trip, I opened my phone on the subway ride to work. As the phone came to life, a picture from an earlier Iceland trip filled the phone's screen. The phone was not programmed to display a picture when I turned it on. It had never done it before. It has never done it again. The thrill that always comes with the recognition that God is communicating across the veil passed through me and I smiled – thank you, Father. I took a screenshot of the Iceland picture and sent it to Alice with a text explaining that the picture had spontaneously appeared on my phone. "Looks like we are going to Iceland," I concluded. I was seventy percent certain now – my faith in interpreting signs always a little hedged, no matter how clear they seem – that we would make the trip. One less thing to worry about.

I was entering a new phase in my spiritual walk where God's love and presence would become more evident than ever before, and my trust in God's care consequently deepened. As the psalmist promised, although I would walk through the valley of the shadow of death, God would be with me, and He would comfort me.[22]

The most remarkable sign of God's presence and care in those early days after the diagnosis happened when I went to Sloan Kettering for my biopsy. I had a biopsy on my second round in 2009 and knew it wouldn't be painful. I wasn't worried about the procedure, but as they wheeled me into the biopsy room I didn't remember the operating theater being so big and high tech. This one looked like a Pentagon situation room. There were huge monitors high on the wall displaying my chart information and vital signs. Dim shapes moved behind elevated smoked glass windows. Presumably they were the interventional radiologist and radiology techs who would guide the biopsy needle into the tumor.

Two surgical nurses fussed around the cavernous room, setting a tray with supplies and adjusting my position face down on the table beneath a robotic biopsy arm. One of the nurses told me she would administer my anesthesia through the IV in my arm. I beckoned her in close and quietly told her that many years before I had abused drugs and alcohol. I was told, I said, that substance abuse had permanently changed my tolerance for anesthesia and could affect my dosing.

The nurse seemed unusually interested in the news of my substance abuse. "How long has it been since you used?" she asked quickly.

"Twenty-nine years," I said.

She looked from side to side to see if anyone could hear her, then stepped close and pretended to adjust my pillow. "Are you in recovery?" she asked sotto voce.

"Yes."

"Me too," she whispered excitedly into my ear. "Almost a year. Isn't it great!?"

I smiled. Hello, God. "Yes, it is. I've had an amazing life. I'm married to a wonderful woman for twenty-five years. We have three great kids. I've had a terrific career. It's been an unbelievable ride." As I said it, as much to myself as to her, I realized how true this all was and filled with gratitude.

"Wow," she said. "Twenty-nine years."

"Just keep going to meetings and do the stuff," I said. "You'll get there."

She grinned broadly, glowing that singular glow you see in AA when someone who has been trapped alone in a very dark place for a very long time feels God's light shining on them, and then she went back to work. I smiled at God's handiwork too. Here, as I was about to get a biopsy for metastatic cancer and could easily have slipped into self-pity, God gave me a reason to be grateful. The nurse's newcomer's excitement at being so recently freed from the hell of addiction and her gushing at what an unimaginable gift twenty-nine years of sobriety must be had filled me with warm appreciation for the blessing my sober life has been. Our secret AA gratitude meeting in the biopsy theater of Memorial Sloan Kettering hospital was as big a miracle to her in early sobriety as the Richmond bellman's breaking his anonymity with me had been in mine. She would talk about it for the rest of her life. She injected my IV with the anesthetic and I went down peacefully, although it did take a second dose to put me under because of my historic tolerance for sedation.

That encounter with the nurse before my biopsy shifted my response to my diagnosis ever since. There have been moments of honest and unavoidable grief, but the overriding theme of the months since her angelic inflection of my story's arc has been gratitude. Through her, God let me see that while the end is coming sooner than I expected, the story of my life in sobriety has been beyond my wildest imagination. I couldn't have dreamed big enough to envision the life God would give me after such an ignominious start.

When Alice and I finally saw Dr. Voss the week before our Iceland trip to get the full diagnosis and treatment plan, I had a shudder of recognition as we stepped off the elevator. I had been here before, with my cousin Chele. She came from Philadelphia to see if there was anything Sloan Kettering could do to reverse her late-stage uterine cancer. Sitting in this same waiting room, I saw Chele and her husband Dave emerge crestfallen from their meeting with the doctor. There was nothing to be done and she died a few months later.

Doctor Voss gave us the news that I had a Stage Four metastatic recurrence of my papillary cell kidney cancer. Now the kidney cancer was in my lymph nodes and liver. It was too widespread to treat with surgery or radiation. The collateral damage from either would kill me. There is no effective chemotherapy for kidney cancer. My cancer was incurable.

While it was incurable, Dr. Voss quickly added, it was not untreatable. There was a new "targeted" treatment combining two drugs, one oral and one intravenous, that stalled tumor growth in sixty percent of cases. If it worked for me, I might have a period during which the tumors did not grow. For those for whom the drug worked, the median length of tumor cessation was six months, although it had worked for several years in some instances. If the targeted therapy didn't work for me, the normal progress of this cancer would kill me in six to nine months. Dr. Voss said that we could – and should – make the trip to Iceland. In the meantime, the hospital would work through the insurance approvals so that I could begin treatment when we returned.

Stop here, as I did then, and consider what brought me to this point. Sloan Kettering cleared me three months earlier at my annual check-up. There was no reason for me to see a doctor until the next year's follow-up exam. Without the rib x-rays, I wouldn't have known about the tumors until they had wrecked my liver function. At that point, nothing could have been done. My liver would have already hit the tipping point and I would have gone from healthy to dead in a month or two.

Instead, we discovered the metastases in time to try the new treatments because a planter I built a decade and a half earlier chose this moment to fail and clog the drain so that I could break my ribs trying to clear it, and even then, it would take a second x-ray at my acupuncturist's request after the urgent care x-ray showed nothing out of order to expose the tumors. All these factors aligned to alert us to the tumors before they became symptomatic, giving my family and me the chance to adapt to my terminal diagnosis over months or, if the medicine worked, perhaps even years of relatively good health, instead of having to deal with it out of the blue amid a suddenly cascading health crisis. That is, I can assure you, an incredible Godsend to all of us. My early diagnosis could not have occurred if God had not once more bent the probabilities to allow it, just as he did sixteen years earlier with Matthew's guided missile that granted us all the good time since. Once again, I knew from the start of this new journey that God was with us, easing our path as He could.

After the glimpse of the afterlife my mother had granted me, I wasn't afraid of death, although the process of dying remains a little scary. Spirituality eases the fear, but I don't expect it to extinguish the fear entirely. That's asking too much. Jesus had far more reason to be confident about the afterlife than me, but He still dreaded entering Jerusalem when His time drew near and He wept tears of blood in the Garden of Gethsemane when His physical torment was imminent. I conclude from Jesus' example that no degree of faith – not even God incarnate's – can be expected to wholly lift my fear of the pain and sadness that may accompany my passage from this world to the next. As I had been reassured by the story of Paul and the thorn in his side that illness is not inconsistent with faith, the way Jesus agonized over his coming passion affirmed that having a little fear about my final illness was not a sign that my faith is weak. The giants of my religion, even God Himself in human form, shared it. Faith could mediate, but not eliminate, that fear.

In the meantime, I wasn't in the Garden of Gethsemane yet. I wasn't even in Jerusalem. I just knew that I was probably going there in the relatively near future. God's reassurances that it would be alright to walk through the valley of the shadow of death seemed to be everywhere as we adjusted to this radical change in my life's presumptive path.

Shortly after getting the initial x-ray report, I left for work late after a rough night of waking regularly from broken rib pain into worries about how my death would impact the family. Still stewing, I sleepwalked down my block toward the R train station. As I passed Matthew's friend Wiley's house, Wiley emerged through his door and we nodded in recognition. Many nineteen-year-olds would have avoided the adult encounter, but Wiley joined me for the next ten minutes of my walk. He was smiling and positive. Wiley laughed as he told me about taking his younger brother, a high school junior, to visit colleges, marveling at his brother's haphazard process of discerning which school he would like to attend.

As we parted, I reflected on Wiley's maturity and character. Wiley's father was killed during a family vacation in the Caribbean, struck by an inept jet ski driver as his father snorkeled with Wiley's younger brother. Yet here Wiley was, just a few years after his father's sudden death, already an outstanding young man. His mother Lisa carried on incredibly with the four boys. I saw her from time to time in the neighborhood walking with one or another of them, and more recently, smiling with them as she did.

Continuing on toward the train, I thanked God for timing my departure from the house with Wiley's to show me Wiley's resilience and remind me of Lisa's at the moment I needed to see it. My greatest concern about this diagnosis was its impact on Alice and the kids. But wasn't Alice every bit as buoyant and resourceful as Lisa? Wasn't Alice's life story one of bottomless strength, confident accomplishment, cool intelligence, and enduring faith? Weren't Matthew, Joseph, and Jane each in their own way as grounded, decent, talented, and strong as Wiley? Hadn't I seen that strength and self-discipline in Matthew, the Eagle Scout and team captain with his sights set on West Point, overcoming every setback in his path? Hadn't I seen it in Jane, our warrior, taking on all the challenges of being the only girl in the Brooklyn travel baseball league? Hadn't I seen that depth of character in Joseph, with his empathy and care for everyone around him, his diplomacy, his intellectual curiosity, and his wit? It would be awful for Alice and the kids getting from here to there, but wasn't God reassuring me through this improbable meeting with Wiley that eventually my family would also come through my early passing with their great qualities tempered and matured by this trial?

I was very concerned with the family's material stability during those early days after the diagnosis. Matthew's college tuition was in the bank, but it would be weeks before I could work through the financial planning and research and negotiation with my disability insurers and the firm to know whether we would have the resources to stay in our Park Slope house and keep Joey and Jane in private school. We had been both careful and blessed with our finances, so our financial doomsday scenario was probably closer to most peoples' dream for their children. Alice could sell our Park Slope brownstone at a profit that would enable the family to move to a good house in a suburb with great schools, mortgage free. But people count more than things. If the kids had to move out of Park Slope, how would they take being uprooted from their home and their network of friends on top of losing me? They were lifelong Brooklynites.

God quickly reassured me on that too. Three years earlier, the son of a former Phillies owner with a daughter in Jane's class invited us to see a Phillies game from the owner's box. We finally made plans to go to a game before I broke my ribs and received the initial cancer diagnosis, and we ended up going to the game shortly afterward. As we headed to Philadelphia, there was a tie-up on the New Jersey Turnpike. The navigator redirected us to Route 1, past Princeton. When we got to the Princeton turnoff, we had extra time and detoured to show Joey and Jane our former hometown.

After touring the estate section, Joey wailed, "Why can't we move here? We could have a yard, horses … We could have jousting matches!" Jane echoed him. They thought the high school looked like a college campus. There was a bubble tea shop on the main street. It looked like heaven to them.

So much for my worries about moving. If worse came to worst, Joey and Jane would still have to adapt to new friends, but at least they were warm to a move to a good suburb like Princeton.

After Dr. Voss confirmed that the cancer was incurable, I needed to learn how to talk to the kids about it. I called Mitchell, a counselor who had been very helpful with Matthew as Matt adapted to the stresses of early language development issues that made his grade-and middle-school academics taxing in the hypercompetitive atmosphere of a New York City private school. Mitchell suggested that I talk to the Sloan Kettering counselors on my return from Iceland to get their advice on how to communicate my medical situation to the children. In the meantime, since Matthew was older and would be hurt if I kept it from him that long, Mitchell suggested that I let Matthew know I had cancer again, but not burden him yet with the knowledge that it was incurable.

Dreading the need for that conversation, and carrying the weight of my new terminal diagnosis, I set out with Matthew five days after seeing Dr. Voss for a guided hike in the Eastern Fjords of Iceland. When we finished the hike, we would meet up with Alice, Jane, and Joseph, who were following us to Reykjavik. Our travel to the hike was a bear. We took an Icelandair flight that arrived at Keflavik Airport at midnight. After collecting our bags, we took the airport bus to a stop a mile from a hostel near the domestic airport, then walked to the hostel. It was after three AM when we arrived.

We slept for three hours, then took an early morning shuttle to the Reykjavik domestic airport. There, we met our guide, a sturdy Icelandic woman in her forties, and the rest of our hikers. We flew in a prop plane for an hour across Iceland to the east coast, where we collected our gear and boarded another shuttle van.

On the way to our first night's stay at a rental house in a small village, the van stopped along a hillside to let us hike a bit. We walked in a line that spread because of our widely varying paces, picking our way down a hill to a stream that split around an island with black volcanic crags and mineral-colored bowls of standing water that we rock-hopped through the stream to reach. On the way back, we traversed the top of a dayglo pasture dotted with shaggy Icelandic sheep, with the sun and clouds dappling the ocean rolling below us. Calmed by the exertion and magical landscape, I had the conversation I had been dreading with Matthew. Matthew was lobbying for permission to spend his summer job money on a car when I changed the subject.

"Matt," I said, "my cancer has returned. It's serious this time, but manageable."

It was out. We walked on a few steps in silence. I waited for tears from one or the other of us. Matthew, to my huge relief, remained focused on the goal and promptly returned to making the case for a car. Thank God for teenage self-absorption, I thought. There would be tears on that trip, mine, unnoticed as I walked behind this fine boy and thought about having to be separated from him so soon, but I had said what the professional had told me to say and Matthew was dealing with it OK. He was being himself among this new crowd, talking away, helping with communal chores, being polite, independent, and generally making me proud.

That evening, exhausted from the short night before and ravenous from the hike, I stuffed myself at dinner and almost immediately collapsed into sleep in a bunkroom with Matthew.

I awoke with sharp pain in my chest. It was still light, as it is nearly all night in Iceland in early August, and I saw that it was one AM. I took an antacid but it didn't help. The pain was serious. I lay in bed worrying. Could this be from the cancer? Where exactly is my liver? Could it be a lymph node? Should I try to bail out before we headed into the more remote hut-to-hut hiking? How would I get back to Reykjavik? If I got to Reykjavik, should I wait there or go back to New York? Did I have insurance for a hospital in Iceland? Should Matthew stay with the hike and meet his mother and the younger kids afterward, or should he and I both abandon the hike?

After long hours of stabbing pain and anxiously running the options, I dressed and slipped outside, where it was misting in the four AM daylight. I walked through the village – weirdly asleep since it was already so light – to the ocean, stopping once to retch a little. It did not help.

When the others awoke, I knew I had to talk to one of the two doctors in our party of nine, either the curt Ukrainian-American woman with the ebullient husband and college-age son, or the stocky, outgoing Australian woman in her thirties who had just come from a much more aggressive hike in Greenland where they took turns watching with a rifle for polar bears during the night. Raised by a doctor, I hated to impose on their holiday, but I needed to know what to do and my becoming incapacitated in a remote area would burden the entire party.

I asked the Aussie doctor if I could trouble her with a medical question. She assented, and we stepped away from the others into the bunkroom where Matthew was packing his gear. I told the Aussie doctor that I had a medical condition someone on the trip should know about in case something happened and revealed my diagnosis to her. I told her about the pain in my abdomen. I apologized for seeking professional advice on her holiday but explained that I didn't want to go further afield if whatever I was experiencing might be incapacitating.

The Aussie doctor said that she didn't think the pain had anything to do with my cancer. That brought my anxiety over the unknown implications of my new diagnosis down several degrees, and with her guided questioning it quickly became apparent what my problem was. I had no cardiac history, and, as part of the diagnostic process at Sloan Kettering, I passed an echocardiogram with flying colors ten days earlier. The pain wasn't my heart. I stuffed myself at dinner, shoveling spicy food and chocolate on top of all the extra coffee I drank during the day to overcome the sleep deprivation of our travels into Reykjavik, then conked out, horizontal, immediately after dinner. I was having an acute episode of acid reflux. I'd had reflux before, under similar circumstances, just not this bad. The Australian doctor pointed out that someone was driving our gear from hut to hut, so there would always be road access to the huts if I needed to be evacuated. This was not a truly isolated area where evacuation would take days.

What are the odds that as I set out on this hike worried about the impact of my newly-diagnosed cancer, I would have two doctors in our group of nine, and one would be a friendly Australian with wilderness experience, without an American doctor's primal fear of reassuring a lawyer that his condition was not serious absent a battery of tests? Maybe this was coincidence, but with the regular stream of God bumps flowing through the traumatic early weeks after my diagnosis, including the appearance of the Iceland picture on my phone to signal that this trip would be possible, I saw God's hand in it. An angel had appeared to comfort me when I needed one. The reflux hurt for several days but eventually resolved, helped along by medicine from the Ukrainian-American doctor's kit.

The last evening before we finished our hike was glorious, especially after days of cold Icelandic rain and fog. I stretched out in the sun on the pinewood deck of that day's hut, talking with the Ukrainian-American doctor and the guide. My fresh diagnosis was still a massive elephant in my room. Now that we were nearly finished with the hike, I decided to share it with the Ukrainian-American doctor. We had spent days hiking, bunking, and eating together, so it seemed alright to mention it. She was a cool professional and would not take it emotionally. The guide was a cancer survivor and shouldn't overreact.

The Ukranian-American doctor appreciated the gravity of my diagnosis and was able to give me some very comforting information. Her mother, she said, died of liver cancer. It was not a long and wasting travail. Her mother was feeling well until the last week and crashed quickly.

After following my friend Jim M's wife's yearlong decline from brain cancer, cousin Chele's slow and agonizing retreat from metastatic uterine cancer, Uncle Joe's excruciating bone cancer, and Dad's months of incessant coughing and struggling for breath with lung cancer, I was relieved to learn that my final stage might not be similarly drawn out for me or our family.

The Ukrainian-American doctor, raised with Communist atheism, said that she would arrange for assisted suicide if she got terminal cancer. That teed the issue up for me to think about. After a few minutes' consideration, I recognized that my religious beliefs wouldn't permit assisted suicide, beyond perhaps hastening the inevitable with a final shot of morphine in hospice like the one I injected into my Uncle Joe's IV under the hospice nurse's direction to spare my cousins that responsibility. It was clear to me that the tradeoff for seeing my course through its final passion, as my exemplar Jesus did, was the comfort my beliefs have given me throughout my adult life and the assurance of my faith and the vision my mother brought me that on the other side of that passion there would be boundless peace and quiet joy surpassing all understanding.

Once more God put someone in my path who could give me the information I needed when I needed it, if I took the risk of honestly engaging with them. That brief blessed conversation with the Ukrainian-American doctor in the early days of grappling with my diagnosis, like the spontaneous AA gratitude meeting with the nurse in the biopsy room, became another inflection point in dealing with my terminal illness, giving me a much less oppressive vision of my probable end stage to carry with me. God could use even an atheist to convey His comfort and clarity to me.

The last day of the hike was extraordinary. Under bluebird skies, we angled up through a pasture rising beside a fjord. The wind was cool and the sun was warm on my face, perfect hiking weather. I thought of the depiction of the afterlife in *Gladiator*, with its shimmering wheat fields and evening glow. This peaceful, gorgeous hillside was, perhaps, a similar distant echo of Valhalla. It will be good, I thought, and that eased the sting of impending separation that blurred my eyes with tears when I looked up at my fine son striding strongly up the hill ahead of me, talking with the Ukrainian-American doctor's boy. Maybe I would see Matthew again, in some form, in my Valhalla someday. It seems unlikely that a God who loves me so completely and who gave me this family to love in my own imperfect, diluted version of His love for me would not someday reunite our souls on the other side in some mysterious way.

When we returned to New York, Alice and I met again with Dr. Voss and he outlined my treatment. I would take pills every day and have a biweekly infusion. The doctors would manage the side effects with other pills. In three months, I would have a contrast CT to see if the medicine stalled my tumor growth.

I hesitated over the first pills. This was serious medicine and the potential adverse reactions on the information sheet were daunting. Once I started the pills, which I would take for as long as they kept me alive, my body would never be the same: it would always be chemically damaged. I talked with Alice and she was unwavering that I should do whatever I reasonably could to extend my life. Reviewing our conversation later that day, with a childish voice in my head shouting that it was my body to treat as I saw fit, it struck me in a shock of clarity how wrong that voice was. It was not my body, it was God's body. It was not my life to do with as I wished, my life belonged to God. Alice, the soul mate God blessed me with, wanted me to do what I sensibly could to prolong my life. God's will seemed clear. I would treat this body as He would have me treat it, in the way that would best serve Him and the people who loved and depended on me. I started the pills, and two weeks later, the infusions.

When I returned to work in early September after the vacation in Iceland and then our annual trip to the family cottage in the Finger Lakes, my emotions remained turbulent. Setting out for the office one beautiful fall day after seeing the little ones off for school, a wave of grief passed over me. It felt authentic, not treacly like self-pity. I knew the grief had to come out, so I let it. Tears rolled and a sob or two racked me as I walked the mile down the hill to the train. When I got to the station, I was still too unsettled to descend into the subway, so I kept walking toward another station two miles further in downtown Brooklyn. I recognized the parallel to the fine fall day my second wife left twenty-nine years earlier, the day I began to wake up like the prodigal son and see how lost I was during another walk to another train station taken because I couldn't stop crying at my home station.

I crossed the Gowanus Canal on the Union Street bridge and started up the hill into Carroll Gardens. The wave of grief ebbed and my emotions calmed. I paused to admire a 1960s VW van parked next to the sidewalk and someone across the street hailed me. It took me a minute, but I realized the man was calling me by name. I recognized his face but couldn't place him. Buying time as he crossed the street, I asked if the van was his and he said no. He sensed my confusion. "It's Eddy," he said, reaching me and extending his hand.

Of course. Eddy, a contractor, was the father of one of Matthew's grade school friends. Like many parents working in construction and real estate, he had to take his kids out of private school when the housing bubble popped in 2008. Our families had been close, even taking vacations together.

The boys drifted apart once they were in different schools. We heard through the grapevine that after their kids left Matthew's school there was a bad divorce and Anne left with the children. We never knew why they split, but the dramatic suddenness of their marriage's collapse suggested infidelity or domestic violence. Eddy drank sometimes, and intoxication could certainly usher in either of those homewreckers. Eddy's brother did some work in our house for Eddy and had the emaciated look, trembling hands, and vodka odor of a late-stage alcoholic, so there were serious booze problems in Eddy's family.

Eddy seemed glad to see me. He pointed out the house he was working on. He asked about Alice and the kids and I updated him. Reciprocating, I asked him how his kids were doing. He turned solemn. "I don't know," he said, looking down. When he looked back up at me, his eyes were wet. "I haven't heard from them in years. They were mad at me after the divorce. Anne changed their phone numbers. There was even a restraining order."

Seeing how sad Eddy was, I tried to comfort him. "They're growing up, Eddy," I said. "You're their dad. They'll get back in touch with you eventually."

"I'm running out of time," Eddy said, looking down again, then back up at me. "I'm seventy-six years old. I'm a lot older than Anne." I was stunned. I commented on how much younger he looked. I'd always assumed he was my age. He smiled ruefully. I told Eddy that I was glad to see him, thanked him for getting my attention, and we parted. Walking away, I prayed that Eddy might find his way to God, and through God's intervention, reconcile with his family.

As I continued up the hill into Carroll Gardens, I was immediately impressed by the grace of this improbable encounter on a day with such eerie similarities to that beautiful fall morning twenty-nine years earlier when I began my journey home to God. I knew why God put Eddy in my path at this very moment, our first meeting in years. It didn't matter whether my speculation about Eddy's drinking was true. What mattered was that, for me, he seemed like a drinking man's ghost of Christmas future.

No, I would not have the time with my children a longer life would have given me, and that had triggered that morning's wave of grief. But unlike Eddy, thanks to God's grace in letting me live my adult life sober, the time I had with my kids was rich and loving. Notwithstanding a mild dose of the usual, necessary bumps of negotiating their independence as they grew, they were terrific kids. All things considered, I was a pretty good dad. Alice and I loved and respected each other. Our family's relationship was one hundred and eighty degrees from Eddy's fractured relationship with his family.

It was a powerful message. While I would have preferred more time with my children and still dreaded our eventual separation, I could see now that in valuing the legacy a father leaves for his family, quality trumps quantity.

I was given the chance to live my twenty-plus years as a parent imperfectly, but soberly, lovingly, responsibly, and attentively. This was not the way family life went with drinkers like me. Eddy's damaged relationship with his wife and kids was more like where my life as an alcoholic should have gone, if I had kids at all. Only God, running to me when I turned to Him decades earlier, and His devoted servants, who showed me the way home through AA's love, fellowship, and its twelve-step process, had let me be a parent in the first instance, and then let me do it for a third of my life in a way I did not have to regret – unlike Eddy and so many other fathers who never find a working relationship with a higher power and bang through their life on self-will, winding up full of remorse over their parenting as they near the end of their lives.

The unlikeliness of yet another critical encounter with an angel carrying essential information from a loving God reaffirmed my faith. What were the odds that I would randomly leave the house late, decide to pass my station, and keep walking so that I could intersect Eddy, who I hadn't seen in nearly a decade, just as he crossed my path on Union Street? If I walked by his worksite a minute earlier, he would still have been in his car. If I walked by a minute later, he would have been inside the house he was working on. The window for Eddy to cross my path so that he could show me exactly what I needed to see to be comforted in the nadir of grieving my diagnosis was only open for seconds. Chance is an inadequate explanation for our encounter. The odds of our meeting that day are too remote, and the specificity of his message for me in the exact moment when I most needed to hear it is too perfectly tailored to be accidental. Only an omnipotent God's loving grace could make this happen. If a loving God could and would do things like this to comfort me, I thought, He would surely see my family through the pain of my early departure.

As I walked on, a broader sense of gratitude came over me. Unlike Eddy and so many other aging men, I did not have to regret how I spent my adult life. God's love, expressed through Alice, my AA support group and my Christian teachers, brought me through the second half of my life without a list of warped relationships to fulminate over as my time runs out. I made the amends that my sponsor approved my making in the way that we agreed they should be made. Going forward after that, when I realized I had done something hurtful, I usually took the AA route of immediately stopping what I was doing, apologizing, and trying to repair the damage in real time. My personal accounts were current. I was not ashamed of how I had lived. Seeing Eddy, I had a profound appreciation for what a gift this was, both to me and to the people I cared about. The storm of grief passed, and the warm light of gratitude began to shine on me again. Except for a few dark hours, it has continued to shine on me since that day. When the light goes out, writing and editing this recollection of God's miracles in my life rekindles it.

Some of the angels God has used to comfort me as I walk through the valley of the shadow have, like the biopsy nurse, Eddy, or the two doctors on my Iceland trip, appeared briefly at a critical point and then vanished out of my life. Others walk beside me for longer stretches.

I know what it is to be on the other side of these relationships. Sometimes, when people I knew tangentially in AA were going through a difficult passage, I was drawn to form a strong connection with them. In retrospect, it felt like I was called to be one of their angels for a term. One example was the way I was driven to dive deeply into the Christian theology of unjust suffering to prepare to serve my friend Jim after his four-year-old died.

A few years ago, another AA Jim, Jim M., began sharing at meetings about his wife's brain cancer. I knew Jim before this, but not well. By the time Jim's wife got sick, I had been through my parents' and Uncle Joe's passing and I had seen how Christian faith in an afterlife of the spirit, buttressed by the glimpse of it my mother brought me, allowed me to be helpful to people grappling with the end of a life. Jim was a Christian too, so we had a common language and spiritual framework for talking about suffering and death. A couple days a week over the year of his wife's illness, I walked Jim back to work after our noon AA meeting, talking through whatever was happening with his wife and boys.

One of the prouder moments of my adult life, when I had no doubt God was using me as an angel for one of his beloveds, came shortly after Jim's wife passed. Jim called me at work one morning, bereft, from the cemetery monument shop. "Bobby," he said. "I can't decide what to put on Karen's stone. I can't get it right."

I left work and met Jim at the monument shop. Twisted by grief and the indecisiveness of a brilliant academic aware of so many more choices than most of us, Jim could not settle on the perfect inscription for Karen's grave. The exasperated monument shop salesman showed me all the sketches he had drawn to try to capture Jim's concepts.

I was given the words to walk through a decision path with Jim to narrow the choices. Within an hour he settled on the inscription and signed the papers to buy the stone. We walked across the street into Greenwood Cemetery and he showed me Karen's plot. I thanked God for letting me be an angel for Jim, God's devoted son, in a moment of overwhelming sorrow.

Jim, along with a core of other solid AA friends, became my go-to angels for navigating my terminal diagnosis. My sponsor George patiently and lovingly listens to my troubles on our regular calls, hunting for a way to set the day's travails in a positive, spiritual light, giving me a little distance and perspective, or sometimes just empathizing. He volunteered his forty years of high-level editing experience to patiently reshape my amateur attempt to write a book for my children. God used Kieran from my noontime financial district meeting to tell me the story of his cousin's near-death experience, which confirmed the glimpse my mother had given me.

On the emotional day in September 2017 when I met with my law partners to discuss my exit from the firm, I dissolved into tears at the end of our meeting. I left my partners to discuss my departure terms among themselves and stood behind closed doors in another conference room, looking out the window, trying to get my act together. My phone rang. It was my sunny, charismatic AA friend Dion, who turned my spirits around.

A month later, in early October, I went through the same emotional storm after meeting with my clients to tell them I was withdrawing from law practice and ask them to consider working with other lawyers in our firm. Again, I sat in an empty office trying to collect myself. Again, the phone rang. Again, it was Dion. What are the odds? We talk on the phone at best twice a month. The thrill of divine intervention through the immaculate timing of his calls minutes after the two most traumatic meetings in my business career reassured and lifted me. God was near, sending angels to tend to me, as He had with Jesus in the wilderness.

The evening after the difficult meeting with my clients, I was walking our dog under the streetlights beside Prospect Park and put in a call to Jim M. to review the day. He had been through the wringer of terminal cancer with Karen and would understand how hard these goodbyes to my professional life were.

"Jim," I said, "I'm tired of emotional meetings where I tell people who care about me something that makes us both sad. I don't want to live in a Lifetime tearjerker. I want to live in an FX adventure."

"Bobby," Jim replied. "Your emotions are what are letting you realize how much love you have in you and letting the people around you realize how much love they have in them.

"I went to a cancer support group with Karen one time," Jim continued. "It was awful and I never went back, but a guy said something amazing. He said, 'Everyone in this club is in this incredible bubble where we get to experience how much love there is all around us, but no one would ever want to be in our club.'"

Jim said that whenever I could, I should take a respite from the emotional work. "This is very hard," he said, and he surely knew that better than most. It's good to have an angel in your corner to tell you things like that.

The most awful moment since getting the diagnosis was telling then twelve and ten-year-old Joe and Jane about it. While Matt's old counselor Mitchell advised me to soften the gravity of my terminal prognosis when I first spoke to Matthew, he also recommended talking to the specialists at Sloan Kettering about how best to communicate my situation to the kids. When I caught up with the social worker at Sloan after the Iceland trip, he told me not to sugarcoat my terminal prognosis. The sooner the kids knew my cancer was incurable, he said, the more time they would have to adjust to that reality before I passed. We planned to talk with Matthew about my prospects in more detail when he was home for Thanksgiving break. There was a deluge of tears around the table the morning Alice and I told Joe and Jane. Can you imagine having a child who loves you so exquisitely that it hurts look up at you in trembling disbelief and ask in a vulnerable twelve-year-old's voice if you are telling him that his dad will never get better?

After talking to Joe and Jane, I wandered down, stunned, to my regular Saturday morning AA meeting. It's a big meeting but I got called on to share. I described the emotional conversation with Joe and Jane an hour earlier and a wave of grief hit me, wracking me with sobs in front of a hundred people. After the meeting, I was swarmed with people offering love and support. They have continued to offer it every week since, as have the people in the daily noontime meeting in Park Slope that became a fixture for me after I retired on disability in November 2017. In much of my outside world, I have a secret – I am flawed and dying – that separates me from other people. In AA, my secret is out and I am treated like a conquering hero for continuing on without resorting to alcohol, drugs, or despair even though I am flawed and dying.

One thing that I remember from the fog of that Saturday when I shared about telling the kids their dad was terminally ill is how a contemporary of mine and a fixture at the meeting, Lisa, told me after the meeting that her father died of cancer when she was young. Her family kept the severity of his illness from the kids until his death was imminent and they could no longer pretend he would recover. Lisa told me how much she would have loved to have known her dad was mortally ill earlier so that his death was not such a shock. She said my kids had loving parents and would ultimately do fine. Lots of people say that, and I appreciate it, but it's particularly reassuring when it comes from someone like Lisa who lived through losing a parent when they were young.

Because Alice and the kids were burdened with the gravity of my illness and the uncertainty of whether the medicine would buy me more time, the whole family shared in my relief when the October 2017 CT scans showed the tumors static or slightly shrunk, confirming that the medicine was working for me. Instead of a few more months, I might have a couple years or more.

It's funny how the way things are framed affects our perception of them. Alice used this knowledge early in our marriage when she was trying to furnish our house and I was being a cheapskate. She showed me a $10,000 dining room set in SoHo so that I was relieved instead of whiny about parting with $1,000 for a good dining room set elsewhere that we are still gathering around twenty-five years later. If our first news about the cancer was that I had a couple years to live, we would have found that news devastating. Now, after God allowed us to spend four months living with a forty percent likelihood of a timeline measured in weeks, the possibility of my living in relatively good fettle for another year or more buoyed us all.

The frenzied rush to get everything in place for a potential six-month lifespan if the scans went the wrong way had spurred me to finish the hardest transitional work before we got the news in late October 2017 that the medicine would extend my time. When Dr. Voss reported the favorable scans, I had already been through a two-month-long financial analysis to confirm that the kids and Alice would be able to stay in the house and the kids could stay in their school if I left work prematurely. My partners and I had worked through the terms of my withdrawal from the firm and signed a buyout agreement. My clients had accepted the new account managers I offered them. The disability insurance and social security applications were in and approved. Alice and I had updated our wills and estate plans. I had drafted an owner's manual for Alice with all the financials, passwords, contacts, and other information she would need to negotiate my passing and pick up my share of our domestic chores. With all that high-wire work behind us, by the time we learned that the medicine was working I was retired from my law practice and we knew where our cashflow would come from. We could enjoy the gift of this extra time together with the heavy lifting done and our finances secured.

Perhaps unsurprisingly, as we emerged from the crisis stage immediately after my diagnosis into this indefinite period of peaceful security, God receded. God, the perfect model for all parents, is not intervening as dramatically as

He was just after the diagnosis with the miracles of my recovering biopsy nurse, the meetings with Wiley and Eddy, or the Iceland picture appearing on my phone. For the time being, we can move forward on our own. After three decades of observing when and how God appears to intervene in my life, reaffirmed by the way God swooped in when we were truly overwhelmed after my diagnosis, I am reassured that God remains near even when He is not being obviously interventional, and that God will show Himself again when we need clear demonstrations of His loving presence.

Even in this lull in the storm, God still periodically tips His hand. One time came after we realized that I needed to apply for the accelerated death benefit on the firm's group life policy before I left the firm's insurance coverage at the end of January 2018. The insurer would pay half the group life policy's death benefit now, enough for three years of college tuition, if Dr. Voss signed a form confirming that my life expectancy was less than twelve months. Collecting the accelerated death benefit would provide more reassurance that the family will be financially secure after I pass. I knew that most people with stage four metastatic kidney cancer don't live long and that the median time my medicine provided a benefit for patients like me was six months, but hadn't Dr. Voss been as ebullient as a German oncologist can be over my initial scans? Dr. Voss might sign the form, and it was certainly worth asking, but since I seemed to be having such a good response to the meds, I thought I might get a little pushback.

Instead, when I emailed the form to his physician's assistant, she responded immediately that the doctor would surely sign the form, "no problem." That was financially helpful but emotionally deflating. I wanted to believe that I had a high probability of living for a couple of years or more, though no one at Sloan had said or even implied that.

They said that there was a chance I could live that long, and it was something I could hope for, but no one had put favorable odds on such longevity.

When the noontime AA meeting the next day was winding down and no one raised their hand to share in the last five minutes, I took the plunge and shared my disappointment over my doctor's ready affirmation that I had a life expectancy of under a year. The meeting ended, we formed a circle and said a prayer, and people began to put on their coats. The speaker at the meeting, who I had never seen before, sought me out. She was a hard-boiled, straight-shooting hospice nurse from pre-gentrified Brooklyn. She didn't pull any punches when she told her story to begin the meeting. I liked that.

"Look," she said. "I used to be an oncology nurse. Just because you fit a demographic doesn't mean that's how your story goes." She eyed me appraisingly. "You don't look that sick to me."

Thank you, God, I thought. What are the odds that I would meet a credible oncology nurse who could set me back on my feet twenty hours after getting the deflating news from Sloan on my life expectancy? An oncology nurse. Twenty hours later. I would put those odds pretty long. I can't think of another time in thirty years of meetings that I have heard another oncology nurse speak, and if anyone else had raised a hand in that last five minutes, I wouldn't have shared my news to give the nurse the opportunity to respond. No, this was God, elegantly dipping back in again when I really needed divine intervention. It was not an accident.

None of this has been an accident.

2018 – Still Here

A year after my diagnosis, the medicine was more or less holding the line: a little new tumor growth here, a little tumor shrink there, and the main event, my liver lesions, largely static. The crystal ball remained foggy beyond the next three months, but it appeared that I might continue to live in relatively good health for many more months, perhaps even another year or more.

My reaction to my death's delay was surprisingly mixed. I was prepared to die, it seems, but not to continue living in limbo, with recovery unrealistic and my condition too uncertain to make plans more than three months out. My sardonic bride caught the situation well when we were in Iceland immediately after my diagnosis. Seeing that I was admiring an expensive wool sweater in a Reykjavik shop, Alice sidled up next to me, and said, "I don't think you should be buying new *socks* at this point. As a matter of fact, you shouldn't be thinking about a new *toothbrush*." We both cracked up and I bought the sweater, which I wear at least twice a week for spite, but I can never forget that death appeared on my doorstep in August 2017. It hasn't rung my doorbell yet, but it is still out there. It might have sat down on the stoop for a smoke, then pulled out its phone and begun playing video games, but it isn't leaving. How long would it be before it stopped futzing around and got on with its business?

Henri Nouwen, a contemplative modern priest who had a near-death encounter with the divine after an auto accident, describes well the aftershocks of approaching death as a believer in the afterlife, then being given more time:

> In the days following surgery, I began to discover what it meant that I had not died and would soon recover ... I was deeply grateful to know that I would be able to live longer with my family and community, but I also knew that living longer on this earth would mean more struggle, more pain, more anguish, and more loneliness. ...
>
> My main question became: 'Why am I alive; why wasn't I found ready to enter into the house of God;

why was I asked to return to a place where love is so ambiguous, where peace so hard to experience, and joy so deeply hidden in sorrow?'

Henri J. M. Nouwen, *Beyond the Mirror, Reflections on Life and Death*, pp. 49-50.

The Apostle Paul expresses the same ambivalence about God's leaving us to make our way through the flawed and challenging material realm after showing us the boundless peace and joy awaiting us on the other side of death:

For we know that if the earthly tent we live in is destroyed, we have a building from God, an eternal house in heaven, not built by human hands ... For while we are in this tent, we groan and are burdened, because we do not wish to be unclothed but to be clothed instead with our heavenly dwelling, so that what is mortal may be swallowed up by life . . . Now the one who has fashioned us for this very purpose is God, who has given us the Spirit as a deposit, guaranteeing what is to come.

Like Henri Nouwen, Paul resolves that the best response to spiritual homesickness is more service to God for as long as we remain in the material realm:

Therefore we are always confident and know that as long as we are at home in the body we are away from the Lord. For we live by faith, not by sight. We are confident, I say, and would prefer to be away from the body and at home with the Lord. So we make it our goal to please him, whether we are at home in the body or away from it.[23]

"We make it our goal to please Him." In AA terms, we practice our Third Step, remembering our decision to turn our lives and our wills, and by extension, our bodies' duration and the time and manner of our physical decline and death, over to the care of the loving God of our experience. And then, we seek to do His will. Christians entrust our course to a God who knows full well how difficult it can be to live on earth and would not ask us to remain here if He didn't have additional work that only we can undertake for Him on this side before our earthly deployment ends. I find that if I make it my goal to do whatever I think will please God right now, the frustration of uncertainty and the longing for home recede. Death still loiters on my stoop, but I can walk by it and get on with my life.

Pain

On a recent Saturday morning, I awoke into sunlight. The bedside clock read 6:55. Not 1:15. Not 2:20. I slept seven hours straight for the first time in months.

As Alice and the young ones slumbered on, I slipped downstairs to savor the afterglow of the restorative night. The white table in the breakfast nook was alight with low morning sun. After days of dreary November rain and snow, the blue sky was pure tonic.

My stomach was unusually settled. I made a cup of sweet milk tea (my preferred caffeine vehicle since my meds made black coffee unpalatable) and lounged in the sun's radiant warmth. Abstract shadows from the breeze-stirred trees of the park across the street played on the table. It didn't hurt when I swallowed the tea. I felt like the clock had turned back three months, before the second round of cancer drugs introduced a raft of new side effects.

The original treatment regimen ran its course in August 2018, after nearly a year of positive impact on my tumors. As the months passed, my body adapted to it. Tumors started growing and spreading again. My late summer CT scans painted the picture of an abdomen shotgun-blasted with marble-sized metastases.

Being terminally ill with a rare cancer is like being on an NFL team down by ten points at the two-minute warning in the Superbowl. It brings out the oncological equivalents of a Hail Mary pass. Since mid-September, I had been what my Chinese mother-in-law calls a "white mouse" in a clinical trial to test a new combination of anticancer drugs. One, a targeted therapy drug akin to the two I took in my first round of treatment, is designed to interfere with the tumors' blood supply. The other drug is an immunotherapy intended to trigger my immune system to recognize the cancer cells as invasive and attack them.

Until this round of treatment began, my primary challenge was wrestling with the *idea* that I have terminal cancer, along with putting our affairs in order. The miraculous early diagnosis flowing from my broken rib x-rays, and the positive response to the first-round treatment blessed us with a solid year of relatively good health. It created a clear space to process the emotions stirred up by my diagnosis and make provisions for my eventual sickness and death without having to simultaneously deal with all the physical challenges of stage four cancer.

There were side effects to my first-round treatment, enough to stop me from being able to continue working as a litigator or backpacking, but they weren't debilitating. I always had a rash like little mosquito bites on my trunk and scalp, but after all my backpacking, mosquito bites don't bother me much. Dysphonia from the drugs gave me a gravelly, Tom Waites voice. Instead of my usual, soft-spoken lawyer's instrument, I croaked like a smalltime South Brooklyn hood or a whiskey-and-cigarettes rocker (albeit with a third of my old tonal range). It's colorful.

It was weird to have my nasal septum disappear,[24] along with much of my senses of smell and taste, yet that bothered me less than I would have imagined. Chocolate tastes weird. Vanilla is still good. Because of the tumors or the meds or maybe both, I can eat anything I want without gaining weight, which is sweet after decades of counting calories. My energy level dropped a bar or two with the first drugs, but most days I could still walk around, eat what I wanted, do chores, and ferry the kids. These initial side effects never approached the crippling malaise of the hangovers I awoke to several times a week during my drinking years.

Since starting the clinical trial drugs in September 2018, I am no longer dealing primarily with the idea of having stage four cancer: I'm getting a taste of its reality. My cancer is still not symptomatic. The tumors remain too small to crowd out organ function in the squishy plate of chitlins that fills my abdominal cavity, or to press on the few nerves in the region. The side effects from the second-round meds are another story.

I try to keep it in perspective. The side effects I encounter on the clinical trial drugs are nothing compared to the load many elderly people lift every day. Some of the plaintiffs I met – quadriplegics and burn victims especially – endured infinitely more distress, some of them for decades. If this cancer was in a constricted space like my bones, as Uncle Joe's was, each moment would already be agony.

The thing is, I'm kind of a wimp about physical pain. I never had to develop the spiritual or emotional muscles to deal with it. Once free of alcoholism in my early thirties, I had no other chronic illness or prolonged discomfort before this. I was in robust health until my diagnosis, scampering up the five-thousand-foot White Mountains like a sixty-two-year-old billy goat. My two previous rounds of cancer were treated surgically, so the pain came and went in days. I rarely took medication, except "Vitamin I," as backpackers call ibuprofen, one pill a night to reduce the swelling after a ten-mile hiking day so I could more comfortably backpack ten miles to the next shelter on the Appalachian Trail tomorrow. This is all to say that, while a more resilient person might not be daunted by the side effects I've encountered from the clinical trial meds, they sometimes dispirit me.

In a voice I hope will not sound intolerably whiney, let me outline the new reality of my cancer with what my former sponsor Vincent termed "an organ recital," the narration of medical complaints that typically opens older peoples' conversations.

Palmar–plantar erythrodysesthesia, more commonly called Hand-Foot Skin Reaction or HFSR, is the most annoying side effect from the new targeted therapy drug. Its mechanism is too complex for me to understand, but the dumbed-down explanation I received is that the drug leaks through capillaries on my feet, hand, elbows and ears, causing the surrounding skin to develop painful callouses and open sores.[25]

Living in an urban neighborhood where we walk to most of our daily destinations, my smartphone pedometer says I hoofed an average of three to four miles a day before starting these meds. With the pain these sores bring on every step, there are days I can barely clear the block. Open sores on each ear launch a stabbing pain whenever they are brushed. Blisters on my hands hurt when I twist a milk carton cap, door key, or lamp knob.

I can often ignore the side effects during the day, unless they are really flaring. When I try to sleep, they gang up on me. The stinging, constantly runny, and often blocked nose the first drug regimen left me with continues with the new one. With my mucus membranes drug-damaged, my nose dries out at night and closes off.

The nose troubles lead to mouth breathing and awakening to a stuck tongue, cracked lips, and a sore throat. I need to sip water several times during the night to moisten my gob. Some nights, mouth ulcerations bloom. The drug irritates my throat and causes a chronic dry cough.

Any pressure between the pillow and my ears, or dragging covers across the broken skin on my feet, is like bumping a hot stove. Bloating or nausea from the cancer drugs appear periodically. Leg and foot cramps give a striking wake-up call a night or two a week.

I get severe acid reflux from the drugs. The acid seared my esophagus, so food can feel like barbed wire going down. I lost ten pounds since starting this round of drugs. Most nights, I wake up at least once and often several times with burning pain in my chest from the reflux. I get out of bed, sit up on the couch, and take antacids. On a good night, the reflux passes in a half hour, and I can get back to sleep.

The targeted therapy drug jacks up my blood pressure. I take three blood pressure medications to lower it. The blood pressure meds have their own side effects, but they are insignificant compared to the cancer drugs'.

I can generally sleep for two to three hours when I first crash, exhausted, into my bunk. Then, I start waking up from one thing or another every hour or two until morning. The cancer drug that raises my blood pressure has the effect of an extra cup of coffee the day before – just enough stimulation to make it hard to get back to sleep. Sometimes, when one or another side effect rouses me, I'm up for hours. I know that the quality of the upcoming day will turn largely on the numbers I see glowing on my alarm clock on my first nightly wake up. If the clock reads 12:30 and my longest block of uninterrupted sleep that night is an hour or two, I'll be dragging through a long day on the morrow. If the clock says, 4:30, I've had a five-hour sleep block that bodes well.

No matter how I sleep, the alarm still goes off at 7:00 five days a week so I can get the younger two up, fed, and out to school. Even if I didn't sleep much, I hate missing the morning routine. It's one of the few things I can still reliably do for Alice. She is not a morning person like me, but these days she often has to take the bullet.

Notwithstanding a parent's familiarity with sleep deprivation, if I've had several rough nights in a row, I just can't make it out of bed at 7:00. Either Alice gets up, or if she can sleep through my alarm, the kids will occasionally get themselves up and out. The ongoing sleep deprivation impairs my memory and concentration.

In the wee hours, when I can't get back to sleep and end up watching the night slipping away, I'm frustrated that this is not some phase I need to endure so I can feel better someday, like you do when you are treated for a curable illness. I expect life to stay like this as long as I am on the meds. When they run their course and I go off them, it will get worse. I know that healing miracles happen, but the odds are these side effects, or ailments harder to tolerate, will happen again tomorrow and every other tomorrow after that. I can't expect to improve.

Beyond the impact of the physical consequences of my cancer on me, I see what this turn is doing to my family. For the first year, I didn't need much care and could still be useful. Now, Alice must pick up more of the workload (having always carried twice my share) and the kids see me faltering. My loved ones look sad and frightened when they catch me weakened, scared, or in pain. I try not to be demonstrative, but sometimes it's impossible to hide. I know it's not logical, but I feel that I am failing them.

And thus endeth the organ recital.

Against that background, awakening last Saturday at 6:55 after seven-plus hours of uninterrupted sleep was an unprecedented blessing. Sitting at the morning table with my cup of tea, more rested than I had been in weeks, enjoying the morning sun, it struck me that on such a day it's hard to let go of this world. If I felt this good every day, I would be continually waylaid by the sadness of having to withdraw from such a delicious place.

The gift from God, so badly wrapped in all these side effects and the final illness that will follow them, came to me. Little by slowly, God is easing me away from the pleasures of this world and shrinking my role in our family's web of activities. As my ability to enjoy and contribute in this realm ebbs, I can more easily let go of the only world I've known. My family, who loves me and hates to see me suffer, can more easily release me from it. Obviously, I don't like the pain and disability, but I can see how a God who loves me could still allow this suffering for our family's ultimate good.

Since the onset of the physical side of the cancer, I've looked for spiritual teachings that might take the bodily pain away as effectively as they relieved my emotional pain. Encountering the pain in zazen helps to relax and not fight it so much, but I haven't found any spiritual silver bullet that makes physical discomfort pleasant.

If there's a truth about physical suffering to be drawn from the Bible, it's that I shouldn't expect to find a palliative there. Surely Jesus on the cross, crying out to God, "Why have you forsaken me?" didn't have one. Psalm 22, the scripture familiar to Jesus that swam into His consciousness during His crucifixion, goes even further into desperation than Jesus could express with the weight of his body strangling his breath after His legs could no longer support Him:

> My God, my God, why have you forsaken me?
> Why are you so far from saving me,
> so far from my cries of anguish?
> My God, I cry out by day, but you do not answer,
> by night, but I find no rest. (NIV translation)

If God didn't give His beloved Jesus a spiritual talisman to ward off physical pain, I am not surprised that I haven't found one either.

Perhaps I can assuage my groans if I return once more to Paul's advice for dealing with them. Surely Paul, cursed with the thorn in his flesh, beaten, stoned, and shipwrecked, knew pain. He didn't like it either – else why would he have prayed, unsuccessfully, three times for God to spare him from it?

What if, as Paul suggests and as I tried doing for the emotional pain of living with my imminent mortality, I make it my goal to please God during my physical pain?

In that light, I ask you, God, what would please You right now? If I am Your child, and You love me more than I can possibly love my own children, and You see my suffering – if You know, through Jesus, exactly how my physical pain feels – what would it please You to see me do?

It occurs to me that maybe I can find the answer if I imagine how I would feel if I saw my own child suffering this way. What would it please me to see my child do? Take the analgesics the medical people have made available for him? Nap? Call a friend? Read an uplifting book, or if he couldn't read in his state, watch something diverting on the tube? Would it please me to see him share his pain and frustration with someone, perhaps with me? Or, would it please me if he invited me to hold him and stroke his head?

If she was up for it, would I want to see my suffering child get out of the house and spend some time with friends who love her and could put her problems in a spiritual context, who might let her see that everyone suffers sometimes, and she is not alone in her trials? If my child was suffering, would it please me to see her write out what she is feeling to get some distance from and perspective on her pain? Would I see that she might feel better if she did the dishes to distract herself and feel useful -- to "move a muscle and change a thought," as AA suggests?

What would it please You to see me doing right now, God?

Alice and the kids are in the next room happily watching a sappy movie. I think I've written enough for today. I believe it would please You to see me join them.

* * *

Oh, and by the way, a week after writing this, the side effects got serious enough for Sloan Kettering to take me off the drug that was causing them. My complaints resolved within days and I felt good again. I've since restarted the drug at half the dose. So far, I'm doing pretty well.

I was explaining this turn of events to an AA friend who knew I had been feeling poorly from the drugs and checked back to see how I was. "I assumed that I would feel bad every day, until I felt worse," I told him.

He pointed out that this is an alcoholic's default view of every problem. Optimism is not our defining characteristic. When an ordinary person's car breaks down, a joke in our circles goes, they call the garage. When an alcoholic's car breaks down, they call the suicide hotline. God and AA have brought me a very long way, but I do occasionally revert to form.

GRIEF AND SELF-PITY

As the last chapter illustrates, I am no stranger to self-pity. Perhaps the most helpful insight God granted me in this round with cancer is how to distinguish self-pity from grief and deal with each appropriately. Knowing that lets me enjoy the time I have.

In contrast to self-pity, grief is unavoidable. Christian teaching offers no panacea for its anguish. We are taught that even God incarnate wept when confronted with the sadness of loss.

> When Mary reached the place where Jesus was and saw him, she fell at his feet and said, "Lord, if you had been here, my brother would not have died." When Jesus saw her weeping, and the Jews who had come along with her also weeping, he was deeply moved in spirit and troubled. "Where have you laid him?" he asked. "Come and see, Lord," they replied. Jesus wept. [26]

In that story, Jesus knew that God would soon restore his friend Lazarus to life, but still grief must come out: Jesus wept. If it remains trapped inside of us, grief, which originates in love and compassion, mutates into something cold, dark, and malignant.

I saw that happen in early 2018 after I flew to Ohio to visit a friend, our church's former pastor, who was dying of colon cancer that had metastasized into his liver. I knew the trip would be hard, especially since liver failure will probably finish me off too, but I thought that I could be helpful to my friend's family, and I believe that I was.

God gave me some useful information on that trip. My friend was mostly sleeping, which spared him from continual awareness of his wasted state and his inability to speak intelligibly. He was not in terrible pain. This was comforting for someone expecting to be where he was before long. God was being merciful to him.

I also got to see how extraordinarily difficult it was for my friend's wife as she tried, without training in transfers, bathing, feeding, or changing an infirm patient, to care for her husband's unceasing needs, while simultaneously juggling household necessities and a stream of visitors, all under the weight of her own heartbreak. I don't know if my friend had the option to do hospice care outside of their home, but it was clear to me that if I could, I would spare my family the unrelenting trauma of at-home hospice care.

I saw the anxiety caused by our culture's sentimental notion that people must make it to the bedside before death. In TV and movies, that's when a deathbed resolution magically heals a warped relationship so we can feel good through our tears when the credits roll. It seems plain to me that relationships don't turn on a dime like that in real life. In real life, good relationships are resilient. Whether there is a final meeting at the end doesn't change anything about the love on either side. For some, like my parents, it was easier to slip away when the people they loved most were not in the room to hold them back.

These were all good lessons, but it was a hard visit nonetheless. Instead of experiencing the grief that arose from seeing my friend's decline and then hearing of his death three days after I visited him, I shut down for the next few days, capping a thick layer of ice over my grief. I was gruff, mean, and unsympathetic to people I saw as getting lost in soupy emotion over my friend's passing.

I continued to be surly and seemingly unmoved by my friend's death until I went to church the following Sunday and heard other people speak who were close to our former pastor. Like Jesus returning to his friend Lazarus' home and seeing Lazarus' sister Mary and those with her weep over Lazarus' death, I immediately connected with my fellow parishioners' sadness. As with Jesus, no thought preceded the expulsion of my grief. Grief is a physical response. It comes from the belly, not the head. I began sobbing and wept for ten minutes. A sudden summer thunderstorm after days of sticky heat, that abrupt cloudburst cleared the air and washed out the entombed grief that was poisoning me. When it passed, I was settled and my baseline empathy returned.

I experienced perhaps ten or fifteen waves of grief in the early months after my diagnosis confronted me with the loss of the future I expected and I saw how sad that loss made the people who loved me. There were the sobbing paroxysms that overcame Joey, Jane, Alice, and me when Alice and I told the little ones that I was incurably ill. Grief came again as I concluded the meeting with my law partners to end our thirty-year business association. It came at the end of the meeting to say farewell to clients who had been friends and supporters for decades. A storm of grief moved through the morning I could not get on the train and ran into Eddy. I let the grief flow freely when it came, and for the most part it has passed as my family, friends, and associates have adapted with me to our new story arc. And each time grief came, God sent angels to comfort me.

In contrast to grief, which begins in the belly, I have noticed that self-pity begins in my head, with words. Now, months after the grief moved through, I might be having a great evening with my kids. I might be watching a sweet movie under a blanket on the couch with a kid's head snuggled on each shoulder. I might be filled with love and gratitude for the gift of this extra time with them. Then a thought intrudes: "You are going to die and break their hearts." I am pulled out of that blissful scene into a dark place in the future. My eyes mist up. I try to hide it from the kids. I am no longer with them.

Self-pity is not natural, necessary, and cathartic like grief. Self-pity is manufactured. It doesn't heal like grief. Self-pity steals. From a Christian standpoint, we know the one who brings self-pity to us. He goes by many names in the Bible: the tempter, the deceiver, the accuser, the father of lies, the lord of the flies, plain old Satan. In AA, we call the "cunning, baffling, and powerful" spiritual malevolence who does this to us "alcoholism" or "our disease." Whatever we call that dark power, it talks to us, in the voice we think of as the voice of our own reasoning.

The most famous example of how Satan speaks to people is in the story of Jesus in the wilderness. That story also holds the key to how we should respond when that voice, whatever we call its source, whispers in our ear.

> Then Jesus was led by the Spirit into the wilderness to be tempted by the devil. After fasting forty days and forty nights, he was hungry.

> The tempter came to him and said, "If you are the Son of God, tell these stones to become bread." Jesus answered, "It is written: 'Man shall not live on bread alone, but on every word that comes from the mouth of God.'"

> Then the devil took him to the holy city and had him stand on the highest point of the temple. "If you are the Son of God," he said, "throw yourself down. For it is written: '"He will command his

angels concerning you, and they will lift you up in their hands, so that you will not strike your foot against a stone.'" Jesus answered him, "It is also written: 'Do not put the Lord your God to the test.'"

Again, the devil took him to a very high mountain and showed him all the kingdoms of the world and their splendor. "All this I will give you," he said, "if you will bow down and worship me." Jesus said to him, "Away from me, Satan! For it is written: 'Worship the Lord your God, and serve him only.'"

Then the devil left him, and angels came and attended him.[27]

Satan in that story sounds like the voice in my thought stream that tries to steal my most precious moments from me and my family with its entreaties to self-pity. The biblical Satan is said to stalk us "like a roaring lion looking for someone to devour,"[28] waiting for his opening when we are in physical or emotional distress like Jesus was, hungry, tired, and alone in the desert.

Like Satan's attack in Jesus moment of weakness in the wilderness, my self-pity is the work of the father of lies coming to me in difficult circumstance to lead me away to a barren fiction of his own creation. As I study his bleak tableau in my mind, he stands next to me, trying to persuade me to steep in sadness over God's failure to satiate my greedy desire for an unending banquet of familial love. If I don't take Satan's bait, I can stay true to the God who loves me in my wilderness and continue appreciating the abundance of spiritual sustenance God has laid before me in this moment, in this warm bath of pure love, with a child's head on either shoulder.

Jesus teaches us that the defense against the tempter's lies comes from the spiritual truths God gives us, whether through inspiration or through scriptures, to expose and answer these deceits. When Satan told me I was an unfaithful Peter, God used the ancient scriptures to let me recast myself as a loyal Paul, given grace to overcome a thorn in my flesh that no amount of faith would remove.

Just when I needed to hear it, our new pastor showed me that it's not just *what* Jesus says to the tempter in the wilderness story that's important for fending off the devil's attacks, it's just as important *how* Jesus deals with Satan. That was a new insight to me and it has made all the difference in successfully dealing with the one who inverts Saint Francis' prayer to bring hatred where there could be love, wrong where there could be forgiveness, discord where there could be harmony, lies where there could be truth, doubt where there could be faith, and despair where there could be hope.

My pastor, the inimitable Willa Rose Johnson, pointed out that in the wilderness story, once Jesus recognized Satan as the author of His subversive thoughts and brusquely dismissed him with a spiritual truth that authoritatively contravened whatever the devil was promoting, Jesus moved on. Critically, Jesus did not engage Satan in a debate or even a conversation. Jesus shut down the exchange immediately and returned from the scene somewhere else that the accuser wanted him to see to the real-world scene in front of His eyes that God made.

Now that I know the melancholy feeling which starts with words and an imaginary vision of the future is not grief and is not necessary or helpful, I can call out the accuser quickly, as Jesus did, then get back to my life. I do not need to keep inspecting the sad deception the father of lies brought me to be sure that I am not stifling real grief. Grief is a different animal altogether. The spiritual tool God gave me on an earlier round with cancer to use when the accuser tries to lure me from my present joy into Satan's depressing visions is to firmly respond to him (in my head, I'm not schizophrenic): "How and when I die is none of my business. That's God's business. How I live is my business and right now I am living." While I had used this line with some success in earlier runs with cancer, I am now much more decisive with it, and it is much more effective.

With the clarity of Pastor Willa's insight on Jesus' temptation in the wilderness, I now know that there is nothing to be gained from dallying with Satan. As soon as I recognize the father of lies as the author of a depressing thought, like Jesus, I draw on God's power to expose and dismiss him, then get on with my business without looking back at the devil to see what else he may have for me.

Part of the joy of being in AA is learning something useful and then bringing it back to the nest to share. Here is how I passed on this lesson in the earthy, universalist language of a three-minute AA share:

> One of the great things about being terminally ill is that people are very nice to you. So, one of my son's friend's mothers invited us to stay with them in their family cottage in Wales. It was beautiful!

> One day I'm walking on a hilltop with my older boy and you can see forever. I was so proud of him. He's really stepping up. And then my disease starts talking to me (I put my hand up next to my right ear, fingers level, thumb and fingers opening and closing to mimic a snake). It says: "You are going to die."

> I was taught to talk back to my disease. I used to be polite about it, you know: "Thank you for sharing. I know you're just trying to protect me, but I'm going to ignore you and do this anyway." Now I'm a lot more direct. It's like (turning to the snake hand): "F*** you. (Turning back to the scene in front of me) This is *awesome*!"

THE LAST SURRENDER

While I think that I have been in God's white light presence a couple of times and I believe that God has communicated with me much more often through signs, scriptures, and part-time angels, I have only heard the "still small voice"[29] of God speaking directly to me twice. Each time, I was forever altered by the encounter.

The first was when I was newly sober and going through my AA steps. The Fourth Step required me to make a written inventory of my actions and attitudes, with the goal of making amends for some of my failings, identifying their root causes, and modifying my behavior going forward with God's help. Part of the process involved writing down the things I had done and the qualities I thought were inherent in me that most shamed me. Then, in the Fifth Step, I had to admit "to God, to [myself], and to another human being the exact nature of [my] wrongs." Following normal practice, this meant I read my Fourth Step inventory aloud to my sponsor.

Before we started, my sponsor said a prayer inviting God to be present, but I experienced that evening primarily as exposing my most shameful secrets to my sponsor and finding that the world did not end. As my sponsor pointed out, none of my sins were original – if they had a name, someone else had already done them. And he helped me acknowledge the reverse grandiosity of pretending that I was singularly terrible. I had messed up, surely, but not in any particularly inventive way. In addition to the faults I so readily found in myself, my sponsor insisted that God must have blessed me with some assets. Humility, my sponsor explained, was not rolling in a mud bath of shame. Humility was having an accurate assessment of my weaknesses and my strengths.

While sharing my darkest secrets with another person was liberating, I didn't feel that I had truly admitted them to God until a couple weeks after doing my Fifth Step, when I lay on my bed with my eyes closed and silently asked God to take the Bob who had done each of my most shameful acts. A still small voice in the middle of my head, clear of all the other mental static, said with reassuring certainty, "Of course I do." Deep inside me, I knew it was true, and the shame I had carried for years was gone, just like that.

The second time I heard God's still small voice was nearly three decades later, on Father's Day 2018. I was morose that morning. Alice and Jane were at Jane's baseball game. I was in church, sitting between Matthew and Joe, an arm around each. I had performed in a gospel concert the night before with a group I helped organize that married rock musicians interested in roots music to our church's stellar gospel singers. There is always a letdown after all the buildup and then the energetic release of a concert. The thought that this might be my last Father's Day with the kids crept in and I kept tearing up.

Children had a big part in the Father's Day service, which made it go on forever. I appreciate children and am glad they have a chance to learn public speaking and participate in worship, but if you are in a crappy mood and the kids aren't your own, it can get tedious.

I was glad when the sermon began. Finally, I might get some spiritual red meat. Pastor Willa preached from one of the healing stories recorded at Mark 10:46-52:

> Then they came to Jericho. As Jesus and his disciples, together with a large crowd, were leaving the city, a blind man, Bartimaeus (which means "son of Timaeus"), was sitting by the roadside begging. When he heard that it was Jesus of Nazareth, he began to shout, "Jesus, Son of David, have mercy on me!"

> Many rebuked him and told him to be quiet, but he shouted all the more, "Son of David, have mercy on me!"

> Jesus stopped and said, "Call him."

> So they called to the blind man, "Cheer up! On your feet! He's calling you." Throwing his cloak aside, he jumped to his feet and came to Jesus.

> "What do you want me to do for you?" Jesus asked him.

> The blind man said, "Rabbi, I want to see."

> "Go," said Jesus, "your faith has healed you." Immediately he received his sight and followed Jesus along the road.

Pastor Willa riffed off Jesus' question to the blind man: "What do you want me to do for you?" Her point was that sometimes we must acknowledge to God what pains us most for God to be able to heal us. She challenged us to try telling God the thing that hurt each of us most deeply.

With nothing to lose, I heeded her suggestion. In my head, I acknowledged to God that the most painful thing for me was the recognition that I would not be able to travel alongside my kids as far as I had hoped to and they would be left fatherless so early. It was a pervasive sorrow.

For months, I had awoken every night out of a nightmare that something terrible was happening to the kids – a fire, a separation in a crowd, an abduction – and I couldn't protect them.

As soon as I articulated my pain over not being able to see my children grow up, I heard the still small voice I had heard twenty-nine years earlier, in the same, static-free place in the middle of my head, beneath all the other mental din. That voice, with all the love and authority in the universe imbued in it, said, "Surrender them to me." Surrender has a big meaning in AA. AA's foundational premise is that, having definitively proven we can't beat alcoholism with our willpower, an alcoholic's only hope is to surrender our addiction to a higher power and allow that higher power, however we experience it, to lift our addiction. Instantly, I knew that surrender was the answer and ceded the children to God.

Again, God spoke and everything shifted. I knew in my soul, no longer just in my head, that the God who loved and cared for me would love and care for my children. God lifted that burden – the weight of wanting to do what I would not be able to do for the kids – almost completely with that single exchange. The transformation reached my deepest psychic architecture: the daily nightmares of not being able to protect the children ended that day and have rarely returned.

When we left the church after services, God immediately reassured me with a confirming sign that my surrender and His care were real. As we wandered home through the annual Seventh Avenue street fair, me trailing Matthew and Joe, I marveled at tall Matthew with his arm draped reassuringly over Joe's shoulder and saw how Joe would be cared for. God would see that there were solid, caring older men, Matthew first among them, to tell Joe how to go on a date, how to choose a college, how to define and defend his standards, how to buy a car -- just as

Alice would continue to be the perfect female role model and mentor as Jane felt her way toward adulthood. God would do what I would not be able to do, in creative and ultimately perfect ways I could not imagine.

THE ANGEL ON THE BEACH

I am tearing up just thinking about this miracle, but here goes.

I did not have to go very far into AA's self-inventory to realize that I was incapable of maintaining a romantic partnership. For starters, there were the two divorces in the three years before I got sober. Behind those, a continuous line of fallen dominos stretched back to my first middle school crush.

My first sponsor sized up my relationship pattern with uncanny precision. "Two needy people," he said, "are drawn together by infatuation. They cling to each other desperately, until one or the other starts to feel suffocated. The one feeling suffocated pulls back to get some air. The other one, sensing a threat to the relationship in the first one's withdrawal from their total immersion in each other, panics and holds on twice as tightly. The one who pulled back feels smothered by the redoubled clinging. The clinging one sees the first one still struggling to withdraw and doubles down again, holding on tighter and tighter, trying desperately to restore the relationship to its initial blind crush. Finally, the tension between the one squeezing like a python and the one trying desperately to fight free of that throttling bind overheats and the whole thing explodes." That pretty much summed up all my romantic relationships from the eighth-grade girlfriend through the disastrous second marriage that led me to AA. Every relationship began its inevitable march to failure with "two needy people, drawn together by infatuation."

Taking my home AA group's advice to avoid major relationship changes during the psychic tumult of my first year of sobriety, I committed to stay out of any new romance until I was sober for twelve months. During that time, I focused intensely on AA's twelve-step process, getting in shape, and Zen meditation. I sought counsel from a psychiatrist to sort through my relationship issues.

I learned some essential things about romantic relationships during that period of abstinence and observation. First, I learned that having an infatuation does not mean that God just presented me with my soul mate. Having an infatuation means only that my instinct to preserve the species has been triggered by proximity to a prime physical specimen likely to produce a healthy heir, which sets off a befogging hormone spray. That fog bewitches me into envisioning that this physically attractive woman is the perfect one and only for me – I must make her mine or perish of loneliness from the missed chance at uniting with my one true love. The books, movies, plays, songs, and TV shows I grew up on continually reiterated this leitmotif.

Now that I could see infatuation as just another strong emotion like rage that leads to bad decisions, not an imperative from God to make the woman in front of me my life partner, I realized that the best action I could take in the grip of an infatuation was inaction. By not acting out on infatuations, I learned how they pass (in about ninety days for me) and it seemed that would be true whether I loved the woman or not. I saw how the eventual clearing of infatuation's intoxicating blur, when the soft glow of otherworldly perfection hardens into the sharp focus of reality, begat the retreating and clinging-tighter seesaw that undid all my earlier relationships. Sometimes my infatuation wore off first. Sometimes hers did.

I learned that healthy people don't charge headlong into commitment at the first trumpet blare of infatuation. They date first and get to know the other person. Then, as the infatuation lifts and they can see how they really feel about each other, they decide whether to mutually advance or retreat.

I learned that when healthy people date there is no panicked, obsessed drive to bind each other to commitments before the infatuation wears off and they can really see each other. Damaged people attract damaged people, so the women I was involved with tended, like me, to secretly imagine they would never be accepted in the clear light of day. Or, they were addicts like me, surfing the biochemical rush of the infatuation, seeking that rush more than any real relationship. For whatever reason, whether the fear of pending rejection or the attraction of another rush, my relationships always ended cataclysmically in infidelity as either I or my opposite preemptively began the search for the next one as soon as the infatuation began to wear off and the end of our relationship loomed.

I came to see how fear and addiction had always driven me from one relationship headlong into the next. I had never taken a break like this to find out whether being on my own would be as devastating as I imagined. During the period of abstinence, learning, and repair in early sobriety, I made the earth-shattering discovery that I could be reasonably content without a romantic relationship. Instead of putting all my emotional investment in one person, I learned during the hiatus in romantic relationships to diversify my emotional portfolio, getting little bumps of love and companionship from a broad web of friends, mentors, mentees, and colleagues. We were a huggy crowd, offering little physical reassurances whenever we met. For the first time, freed of my old predatory drives, I could enjoy a meal or a walk or a movie with platonic women friends.

After a year on my own, I was a holy man. I was sitting zazen, going on meditation retreats, exercising aggressively, doing service in my twelve-step group, attending to my job. I began to think that I had evolved beyond the pedestrian urge for a mate that wrecked so much havoc in the lives of the less enlightened.

Others did not fully appreciate my spiritual attainments and hinted that I was becoming insufferable. My friends, my sponsor, and my shrink encouraged me to start dating again. My unsentimental shrink told me to "get out into the lab, make some mistakes, see what you've learned."

With all this good counsel, I timidly accepted a female friend's invitation to meet her girlfriend. There were no initial sparks, which I took as a good sign. We had a lunch and a dinner. We went to a movie. I had never moved at such a languorous pace with an eligible woman. My alcohol and need-fueled relationships demanded velocity – there was no time for this "she loves me, she loves me not" investigation. In the past, I couldn't bear not knowing immediately which it was.

The woman was, as the friend who introduced us promised, a nice person, but after three or four dates there were still no sparks. I asked my advisors what to do. "You meet with her and gently tell her that you don't see the relationship going further but you appreciate her and her friendship," they all said in one way or another. This seemed like a mature and horrible thing to do. What if she started crying and begging me to stay?

We scheduled another dinner. I was so agonized over how to begin the suggested conversation that I had to excuse myself to deal with a roiling belly. Drained, I trod back upstairs from the lavatory to the dining room as if climbing gallows steps. It had to be said, and it had to be said now, and it had to be said by me. I was embarrassed by how long I'd been gone as I smiled wanly and slid my chair back to the table. I looked up and took a deep breath, but she interrupted me.

"Bob," she said. "You are a really nice guy, and I've enjoyed getting to know you, but I don't see our relationship going any further." She was dumping me! Reeling from the ego blow, I mumbled agreement and muddled through desert. Outside the restaurant, she kissed me on the cheek, the entirety of our physical relationship, and headed off.

"Wow!" I thought on the train home. "This is what normal people must do!" Instead of drinking someone you've just met out of a bar, spending a clumsy night together, and if you were both still infatuated the next day, spending every possible moment together until the panicked ebb of infatuation begins a few weeks later, you could just get to know the person and if they weren't the one, no one had to get hurt! It was an incredibly novel and liberating epiphany.

Months after that first adventure in sober dating, despite another responsible date here and there, no new romantic interest developed. Hoping to end my monkish existence, my best friend Ruairi, the Irishman who had been put in my apartment to paint it with Chuck and who reappeared at my first AA meeting, began planning a spring vacation with me in the Caribbean. Riding the train home to Westchester from Manhattan each night, we poured over the tourist guides and discussed our options.

We settled on Saint Martin. Ruairi wanted to stay at a nudist resort. "Bob," he said in his well-born Dublin brogue, "the Scandinavian girls favor nudist joints. They luv ta strip off." Ruairi had made something of a sensation by stripping off at Rye Beach when his parents first moved to the States, not realizing that prudish Americans had a more restrained view on public nudity. My opinion was that the nudist resort would more likely be populated by gay middle-aged European men. Ruairi reluctantly surrendered the nudist resort plan, and we ended up booking a room in a guest house on the beach in Grand Case, a less than grand – in fact, sleepy and slightly decrepit – beachside hamlet on the French side of the island. We visited the nudist resort when we got to St. Martin and did not see any Scandinavian girls, just paunchy middle-aged men with leathery tans and big sunglasses.

The feeling that something was stirring began on the flight down. Ruairi and I were in a bulkhead row, just behind the exit door at the front of the coach section. One of the flight attendants was particularly attendant to us. She was not unattractive, in a dissipated sort of way. We could smell her stale cigarette odor when she leaned in to talk to us. Broken veins were beginning to spiderweb her cheeks. In my drinking life, she would have been my kind of girl: wounded, addicted, needy, probably promiscuous. I had never gotten so much consideration from a flight attendant. It was flattering.

On final approach, she strapped into a jump seat by the exit door facing us. She asked us where we were from, what we did, where we were staying, and for how long. There was a familiar hunger about her. I spent decades living with its insatiable push and was still instinctively drawn to it in her.

As we exited the plane, she handed me a piece of paper with an address and phone number. "This is where we're staying tonight," she said. "Why don't you come over?" The way she asked made clear that the invitation implied more than small talk and parlor games. Drinks would be served and everything was on the table.

Dumbstruck that a movie could be playing out like this with me cast in the role of the young buck pursued by a stewardess, I tried to smile and pocketed the number as she shifted back to smiling courtesy to thank the passengers behind me for flying with her airline.

I didn't really think I should go, being the new man that I was, but still – a dissolute flight attendant after more than a year of abstinence? On the other shoulder, my better angels chided that she looked like a heavy drinker and nothing healthy could come from this. In more tangible form, there was Ruairi. I showed him the slip of paper and smiled. We had been invited to a stewardess party. The mind boggled. He studied the slip of paper for a second as we strode through the airport toward baggage claim. "Do ya tink diss is a good idea?" he asked, smirking under his fallen bangs. "She looked a bit of a wreck." No, I didn't. I dropped the paper with her address and number into a trash bin and walked on through customs to baggage claim.

I felt like I had passed a test. I had been given the chance to go back to the pigsty I'd come from, to restart the whole messy cycle of velocity and hurt and need again, and I'd not taken the bait. Get thee behind me, Satan.

We both hoped to meet Miss Right on the trip, Ruairi perhaps less so than me (I think he might have settled for Miss Right Now), and he had held the possibility of Cupid's arrow finding me in St. Martin out as inducement when we were debating whether to go on vacation together. "You've got to get back in circulation if you're going to find a mate," he urged.

The only place where we knew how to meet women on vacation was in bars. As recovering alcoholics, we felt iffy going to bars, but if we were going to socialize with women, it seemed our only option. There were female vacationers in the bars we visited, hounded mercilessly by the French locals, but they wanted nothing to do with Ruairi and me. It was weird. I lacked the confidence to be a lothario, but while I felt obligated not to believe it, I was pretty good looking in my youth. Ruairi was unquestionably dashing with his Trinity College bearing, bright Irish wit, and that killer brogue. I knew at least three women in our circle who had crushes on him. And we were sober in a bar – polite, not pushy or aggressive, just friendly. At a bare minimum, the American women should have been talking to us as a safe harbor from the crush of carnivorous, drunk Frenchmen swarming them. We sipped our cokes and tonic waters, studied the scene, chatted with each other, and said hello to nearby women when the opportunity arose, but nothing came of it. Not even a conversation. It was weird.

And the next night, a different bar but the same thing. No women would talk to us. The third night, the same. We had to amuse ourselves watching a local man who appeared in the bar the first night, flush with cash from winning a cockfight, buying rounds and loudly demanding attention, as he came unwound over the ensuing three-day cocaine binge. By the third night, eyes darting, unshaven, his shirt and shoes gone, his pants torn and filthy, dried blood crusting his nostrils, he darkly and loudly fulminated in Creole at the end of the bar as the other patrons gave him a wide berth in deference to his barnyard odor and evident madness. There but for the grace of God ...

The next morning, as Ruairi slept in, I prayed and meditated, and then it struck me: God was not going to encourage me to hang out in bars, and without God's help, I was not going to meet my mate. I acknowledged then that this would not be a trip for meeting mates, as much as I had secretly watered the seed Ruairi planted that it would be. I had to let go of that idea and leave it to God when and where and if I would ever meet a mate. This would be a different vacation. This was a vacation for rest, renewal, and recovery. We would get in touch with the local AA community. I would meditate, exercise, read. And in God's time, some other time in some other place, if I was ready, I would meet someone. And if I didn't, I would continue to be, as I had learned over the last year and a half I could be, reasonably content without a mate.

I went out to the sheltered bay in front of the guest house for a swim. It was a lustrous blue Caribbean day, with light winds and puffy clouds. I put on dark goggles, waded into the sea, and began a long, slow crawl fifty meters offshore to the end of the bay and back, relaxing into the rhythm of my stroke in the warm water and sparkling sun. On my second lap, as I rolled my head with every other righthand stroke to breath, I glimpsed a covey of young women on the beach. On the next righthand stroke, I counted three or four of them. They seemed fit and cute, at least from a one-second peep moving past them fifty meters out. They were out of sight behind me by the third time I rolled my head to the right to breath.

My mind began to spin. Should I try to meet them? How would I do it? I remembered how the women in the bars responded and my fragile confidence flagged. I tried to push back against the fear, but then stopped. I remembered that I had learned my lesson. This trip wasn't for chasing women. I had turned the question of finding a mate over to God just a half hour before.

Once I resolved that I didn't have to approach the women on the beach, the adrenaline ebbed. I tried to forget about them and enjoy the clear water, the strength in my body, the warm sun on my back. When I swam past the women on the beach on my return, they were on my left. I didn't alter my stroke to look at them and contented myself with the sun sparkling on the sea out to the horizon and the distant boats plowing furrows across it as I rolled to my right to breath.

I returned to the guest house and showered the salt water off my skin and hair. Ruairi, a champion napper nursing his body back to health from a severely misspent youth, was still sawing logs. I dressed and went out for coffee and fresh buttered bread at the Portuguese bakery across the street. I was mildly infatuated with the married proprietress and looked forward to having at least one attractive woman on this island smile at me as we exchanged francs for bread and coffee, which she did.

Another pretty woman at the bakery smiled at me too, a young Asian woman with glasses who might have been in the covey at the beach. I hope that I smiled back politely, but I was too flustered to remember now if I did. My mind started to spin again. Should I say hello? But no. I cut it off. This was not a vacation for trying to meet women. I turned away and sat down at a table in the gated patio with my bread and coffee, facing the beach.

Later that afternoon, Ruairi arose and we executed on our plan to attend an AA meeting. It had taken a while to find it. Two days earlier, Ruairi, who claimed to speak French, inquired at a police station on the French side of the island whether there was a local Alcoholics Anonymous meeting. "We have plenty of alcoholics," the gendarme at the desk responded, "but they are definitely not anonymous." We finally called the New York City AA Intergroup office – this being years before the internet – and learned of a meeting in Phillipsburg, on the Dutch side of the island.

We put the canvas down on our little Suzuki rental jeep since the afternoon remained sunny and warm. As we pulled onto the road to Phillipsburg and pointed the jeep toward the AA meeting, we saw the Asian woman from the Portuguese bakery again, now with some of her friends, hitchhiking. They would be safe with us, but we couldn't say the same for the drivers behind us. Chivalry demanded that we stop for them.

The young women climbed in the back of the jeep and, my recent resolution freeing me of any nervous-making obligation to try to charm them, we had a relaxed conversation, led by Ruari in the passenger seat, for the half hour drive into town. The women were a bright light after the dark and noisy isolation of the bars. They were smart, funny, and charming. We dropped them in Phillipsburg without any plan for further contact. It was no longer that kind of trip. And besides, they were too young for us, especially for me since I was older than Ruairi. We went to the AA meeting and then looked for a place for dinner.

Phillipsburg is a small town and we bumped into the women again. They had not eaten and were happy to join us since we had jobs and money, which, it turns out, they did not. Still freed of the obligation to be suave by my recognition that I was no longer chasing girls on this trip and that these women were too young for me, I simply reveled in their bubbly company. After we ate, we all went to a disco where I tried to dance. I don't remember whether we drove them back to Grand Case or if they stayed out in Phillipsburg.

During the initial jeep ride, the women reported that they were seniors at Bryn Mawr on a final spring break trip before graduation. During dinner, they revealed that their trip was lightly planned and severely undercapitalized. They were sleeping in a back room behind a bar, two to a bed. Food was barely on the budget. The French were on them like hounds to a fox, so we were the perfect companions – safe, pleasant, mobile, and liquid. We knocked around with them off and on over the next couple of days on St. Martin and saw them again on the boat we took to St. Barth. For Ruari and I, their company was well worth a meal or two. We thoroughly enjoyed them. I was most impressed with the Asian woman, but she didn't seem my type. There was a wan, dishwater blonde among them who looked a little tormented. She was more my type, or at least always had been, but I wasn't interested in her. Something had changed.

When it came time for us to leave St. Martin, I gave the Asian woman my telephone number since she was from

New York and invited her to call when she was in town. I did not expect that she would, but Ruari insisted, "You're gonna hear from those girls." And I did, not from the Asian woman, but from two of her friends. They knew a free lunch when they saw one and called me to get one when they came to New York after their Bryn Mawr graduation. They said that Alice, the woman I gave my number to and who had given it to them, wanted to come to lunch too but she had to go to her brother's graduation from NYU.

Alice called later and we made a dinner date. I got to the restaurant first and sat at a table by an open window. As Alice steamed down the street toward me, a little past the appointed time, I saw her blow her bangs out her eyes. She was nervous too. After dinner, we walked around the Upper East Side and she stopped in a shoe store. She studied a shoe in the discount bin intently as she turned it in her hand, rejected it, and we left the store. I knew from the way she studied that shoe that she was serious, practical, and special.

A year later, after consenting to marry me, Alice promptly moved to Hong Kong to work as a foreign correspondent. That taught me something about managing my insecurities. Alice was strong and independent. She loved me, but she didn't need me, and it wasn't entirely clear after a few months that she would come back for our wedding. Thankfully, she did. We've been married for twenty-six years and have never been closer or more deeply in love than now. She has been the perfect mate for me: smart, funny, energetic, passionate, hard-working, and, it turns out, prolific, bringing three extraordinary children into the world, each blessed with their own amazing mix of gifts and talents. Once I recognized that her decision-making was much less fear-based and much more clear-eyed than mine would ever be, I stopped arguing (for the most part) and generally acceded to her suggestions despite my misgivings. This widened and deepened my world and the kids' beyond anything we would have known without her. Alice has been an amazingly gifted and diligent mother to our children. And there I go, tearing up again.

So what are the odds? How likely is it that, completely by chance, less than an hour after surrendering my search for a mate to God, I would meet my true soul mate — on my way to an AA meeting in St. Martin? And since I met her only after I had given up the hunt, I was ready to behave like the decent man I was instead of just another panting pursuer, savoring her company without the pressure of trying to win her over in those first encounters. Given the miraculous timing and circumstances of our meeting, I never doubted that our relationship was God-given, even as we trudged through the sleep-deprived molasses of babes-in-arms.

And since God is not the only spiritual entity who can move freely through time, isn't it interesting that God's opponent, the one who wants us alone, self-absorbed, and miserable so that we are useless to God, would try so brazenly to knock me off course to that fated meeting with Alice by putting his unwitting serf in my path, the poor flight attendant, as lost and blindly enslaved in her own foreign land as I had been in mine, to make her once-in-a-lifetime overture?

The hardest thing about my relationship with Alice has been accepting the gift, believing that this wonderful woman — too young, too beautiful, too healthy, too smart, too principled, too devoted, too brave, too perfect for a guy like me — could be the mate God chose for me and that I could be the mate God chose for her, but we are. John Hiatt has a song about love with the line, "Love don't come from you and me, it comes from up above." I believe that.

Alice and I have had a life together beyond anything I could have imagined. I couldn't dream big enough. With our age difference, it was always unlikely that I would grow old with her. The odds were that I would come to the end at least thirteen years before her and she seems to be aging slower than most, but I had hoped to have more time than this. Still, how can I not be grateful for the time we have been given, for the love deeper and richer and wider and longer than most people will ever experience?

And why should I doubt, given the way God has always loved and cared for us, that God will see her through our coming separation with a divine grace and love that will support her and our kids in ways I cannot foresee? Hasn't He always done this? Has God ever abandoned us? Angels will surely appear for them.

And finally, in that we are spiritual beings having a human existence, brought together by God to do things for Him we could never have accomplished without each other, is it too big a stretch to imagine that Alice's and my spirits, and those of our kids, will be together again in the blink of an eye against the space of eternity, reunited with all the other spirits bound in divine love to us, in the place where my mother's spirit, pure and at peace, awaits me?

These are the hopes, which I don't consider unrealistic based upon my experience, that have made death, for the most part, lose its sting. Relieved of the fear of death, but constantly aware of its approach, I have been enabled to live more fully and freely since my diagnosis than ever before in my life. I know that I cannot wander far from God without collapsing into despair, so I have tried harder than ever before to stay close. Because God is the source of everything I crave, the result is that this time – so precious, so charged, so enchanted, and so uncertain – has had a richness and magic like no other.

CLOSING PRAYER

My old sponsor, Vincent, was, he told me, what the Irish call a "spoilt priest." Orphaned at twelve, he graduated seminary but balked at the vows, marrying twice and siring three amazing children. While Vincent lost his faith in Catholicism, he never stopped seeking God, winding up something of a Sufi-Zen mystic. He called his higher power "my beloved." Vincent kept his Catholic appreciation for the value of repeating set prayers and wrote me out a meditative prayer with a fountain pen on an index card, faded now with age, in the beautiful script the Irish Christian Brothers beat into him in 1940s Dublin. It conjures up the best of this time for me:

> Where am I? I am here. And what time is it? It is now. I am here, now, in this, the most precious, the most perfect moment of my life to feel at peace and joyful. Nothing needs to be changed about it. I don't need to be somewhere else, with anyone else, doing anything else. This moment is complete and whole. God please help me to enjoy the gift of this moment with you.

So I pray, as Vincent taught me: Thank you God, for all of it, most of all for your unwavering love and investment in me. Thank you for showing me the bridge back to life when I was lost in a barren wasteland. Thank you for running to me and throwing your arms around me when I turned back to you with the slightest acknowledgement of your possible existence. Thank you for all the comforting signs and signals of your loving presence throughout my adult life, and the revelations you granted me of the wondrous spiritual life that awaits.

I've heard the spiritual path described as a spiral up a mountain. One side of the mountain is in the sun and the other in the shade. If we keep trudging the path when we find ourselves on the dark side, I was told and ultimately found for myself, eventually we come around to the light side again, higher up than we were before, closer to the sun and able to see further. Thank you for withdrawing from me when I needed to walk the dark side of the mountain, and for helping me to stay on the path until I could see your light again.

Thank you for everyone you sent to teach and heal and care for me. Thank you for your angels. Thank you for the problems, which arrived, as Stephen Mitchell put it, "like a letter with my name on it," maturing my faith and edging me closer to you, the source of all my hopes, peace, and joy.

Thank you for the gift of this precious, lingering twilight in the firefly's flash of my human existence, with all its richness and the precious chance it has afforded my loved ones and I to prepare for my return home. Let me continue to be among your hands and your feet on this side for whatever time remains. Protect me from the evil one and all of his snares. Let me stay on the path, Father, all the way home to you. Let me do what you want me to do in this day, say what you want me to say, hear and see and think what you want me to see and hear and think. Please, God, if it's your will, let me see you in this day.

CLOSING PRAYER

Thank you for everything. I have no complaints whatsoever.

ACKNOWLEDGMENTS

I am very grateful to my friends George, Peg, and John for reading early versions of this manuscript and encouraging me to publish it. I am indebted to my former pastor Dale Pauls of Stamford Church of Christ and my current Pastor, Willa Rose Johnson of Greenwood Baptist Church in Brooklyn for looking over my spiritual musings and cheering me on. I am most thankful to Alice for sharing her life with me and for letting me share some of our life together with others. She also fact-checked my recollections of our adventures. My kids have bravely and generously celebrated my literary ambitions notwithstanding the potential mortification of having their Dad say dopey things in public. My copy editor, Theresa Arkenberg, made this manuscript far more correct, readable and lucid than it would have been without her thorough and thoughtful review. If there's a typo or grammatical error, I snuck it in after her last edit.

Cited (and recommended) texts, in order of appearance, are: *Accidental Saints, Finding God in all the Wrong People*, Copyright 2015, by Nadia Bolz-Weber, Convergent Books; *My Bright Abyss: Mediation of a Modern Believer*, Copyright 2013, by Christian Wiman, Ferrar, Strauss and Gireaux; *Life After Life*, Copyright 1975, 2001, 2015 by Raymond A. Moody, Jr, M.D., HarpurCollins Publisher; *Beyond the Mirror, Reflections on Life and Death*, Copyright 1990 by Henri J. M. Nouwen, The Crossroad Publishing Company.

ENDNOTES

---

[1] Christians have long debated whether God has a gender. While the Bible uses the storytelling conventions of the times and places where it was written, my impression is that God is far beyond gender. As the Apostle Paul said, when we enter the spiritual realm, such earthly distinctions disappear: "There is neither Jew nor Gentile, neither slave nor free, nor is there male and female, for you are all one in Christ Jesus" (Galatians 3:28 [New International Version]). God, throughout the Bible, confirms that He is mysterious and beyond our ken. See, *inter alia,* "'For my thoughts are not your thoughts, neither are your ways my ways,' declares the Lord. 'As the heavens are higher than the earth, so are my ways higher than your ways and my thoughts than your thoughts.'" (Isaiah 55:8-9 [NIV]). When I use a masculine pronoun for God, it is not because I believe the incomprehensibly mysterious God can be personified, much less personified as a male. It is simply from convention and because it strikes me as the least pernicious compromise. Using no pronoun for God gets clunky, and interspersing She for He seems only to draw more attention to God's potential gender when I don't believe gender applies to God at all. Similarly, when I refer to God the Father, as the ancient scriptures do, I am talking about God's relationship to us as a template for earthly parenting, equally applicable to mothering. I am again not implying that I believe God has a gender.

[2] AA's avowed goal is to trigger a spiritual awakening that will allow otherwise hopeless alcoholics to stop drinking. Its foundational texts were written in the United States in 1939 (*Alcoholics Anonymous*, the "Big Book") and 1952 (*Twelve Steps and Twelve Traditions*, the "Twelve and Twelve"), a time

when stores closed on Sunday by law to observe the Christian sabbath and courts and schools recited the Lord's Prayer straight from Matthew 6:9-13 because that is how Jesus said we should pray. There was virtually no recognition at the time that this might violate the separation of church and state or justifiably offend the legitimate beliefs of some American citizens. Given the ubiquity of Christianity in mid-twentieth-century America, the Christian cosmology would have seemed unquestionable by almost anyone in that time and place who believed in a higher power. "Up until the 1960s, the 'Protestant establishment' (the seven mainline denominations of Baptists, Congregationalists, Disciples, Episcopalians, Lutherans, Methodists, and Presbyterians) dominated the religious scene, with the occasional Catholic or Jewish voice heard dimly in the background. References to American religion usually meant Protestant Christianity." (Joanne Beckman, *Religion in Post-World War II America.* http://nationalhumanitiescenter.org/tserve/twenty/tkeyinf o/trelww2.htm)

As AA grew, its founders realized that the Christian cosmology underlying AA's foundational texts and its Twelve Steps was not universally accepted. They emerged from their parochialism to see that there could be other legitimate ways of understanding man's place in the universe. Co-founder Bill Wilson regretted his early overemphasis on Christianity as the only path to a higher power, recognizing that it barred the door to people who might have been saved by the AA program, but who, for one reason or another, could not accept Christianity.

> "In A.A.'s first years, I all but ruined the whole undertaking with this sort of unconscious arrogance. God as I understood Him had to be for everybody. Sometimes my aggression was subtle and sometimes

it was crude. But either way it was damaging – perhaps fatally so – to numbers of believers."

A.A. Grapevine article, 1961, excerpted in *As Bill Sees It*, p. 146.

While leaving its original Christian constructs intact in the Big Book and the Twelve and Twelve, AA has tried to make clear through its other sanctioned writings and through its governing Traditions that those Christian constructs should be freely adapted in the most universalist way so that no one suffering in the hell of addiction is unnecessarily prevented from accessing the potentially lifesaving cure God entrusted to AA.

> Newcomers are approaching A.A. at the rate of tens of thousands yearly. They represent almost every belief and attitude imaginable. We have atheists and agnostics. We have people of nearly every race, culture and religion. In A.A. we are supposed to be bound together in the kinship of a common suffering. Consequently, the full individual liberty to practice any creed or principle or therapy whatever should be a first consideration for us all. Let us not, therefore, pressure anyone with our individual or even our collective views. Let us instead accord each other the respect and love that is due to every human being as he tries to make his way toward the light. Let us always try to be inclusive rather than exclusive; let us remember that each alcoholic among us is a member of A.A., so long as he or she so declares.

Bill Wilson from a July 1965 *A.A. Grapevine* article quoted in AA's 2014 pamphlet *"Many Paths to Spirituality."*

In the wonderfully humble language that has come to characterize AA's approach to spirituality and religion, Bill Wilson summed up as follows:

> We are only operating a spiritual kindergarten in which people are enabled to get over drinking and find the grace to go on living to better effect. Each man's theology has to be his own quest, his own affair.

Bill Wilson letter, 1954, quoted in *As Bill Sees It*, p. 95.

3 "Remember that we deal with alcohol — cunning, baffling, powerful! Without help it is too much for us. But there is One who has all power — that One is God. May you find Him now!" (*Alcoholics Anonymous*, p. 58.)

4 The Christian view of the limits of human will to overcome sin and God's power to transcend our limits adopted by AA is stated in this way by the Apostle Paul:

> ... I want to do what is right, but I can't. I want to do what is good, but I don't. I don't want to do what is wrong, but I do it anyway. But if I do what I don't want to do, I am not really the one doing wrong; it is sin living in me that does it.
>
> I have discovered this principle of life—that when I want to do what is right, I inevitably do what is wrong. I love God's law with all my heart. But there is another power within me that is at war with my mind. This power makes me a slave to the sin that is still within me. Oh, what a miserable person I am! Who will free me from this life that is dominated by sin and death? Thank God! The answer is in Jesus Christ our Lord. So you see how it is: In my mind I really want to obey God's law, but because of my

sinful nature I am a slave to sin.

Romans 7:18-25, New Living Translation (NLT)

[5] Luke 15:11-24 (NIV)

[6] I take no issue with those who worship and pray to Jesus as God or as their intercessor with God. Certainly, there is scriptural support (albeit stemming more from Paul than from Jesus) for that practice. I just see Jesus being humbler in describing His relation to the God He prayed to. See, *inter alia,* John 14:10: "The words I say to you I do not speak on my own authority. Rather, it is the Father, living in me, who is doing his work."(NIV); John 5:19: "So Jesus replied, "Truly, truly, I tell you, the Son can do nothing by Himself, unless He sees the Father doing it."(NIV). It doesn't seem to me that Jesus wanted to come between us and a direct relationship with God, but rather that God used Jesus to help bridge the gap human beings had created between themselves and the distant, angry God they imagined.

[7] Exodus 12:29-32, Genesis 19:24-55, Deuteronomy 20:14-16.

[8] Compare, "For God so loved the world that he gave his one and only Son, that whoever believes in him shall not perish but have eternal life" (John 3:16 [NIV]) or, "Jesus answered, 'I am the way and the truth and the life. No one comes to the Father except through me.'" (John 14:6 [NIV]), so often cited on placards in football game endzones to support Christian exclusivity, with the God Jesus describes in the Parable of the Prodigal Son as running to His lost child with no intercessor, or the Pauline vision of God's broad acceptance in Romans 2:13-16: "for it is not the hearers of the Law who are just before God,

but the doers of the Law will be justified. For when Gentiles who do not have the Law do instinctively the things of the Law, these, not having the Law, are a law to themselves, in that they show the work of the Law written in their hearts, their conscience bearing witness and their thoughts alternately accusing or else defending them..." (NIV). See also Jesus' inclusive view that if we see people performing graceful actions, we are seeing God's handiwork in them, irrespective of whether they profess to be Christians. "A tree is identified by its fruit. If a tree is good, its fruit will be good. If a tree is bad, its fruit will be bad." Matthew 12:33 (NLT). I am not trying to convince anyone that either view is definitive, only that Christianity leaves room for an earnest believer to find support for the inclusive view I have found to be more consistent with my experience. I have seen too many miracles of healing in AA nurtured and encountered by non-Christians to believe that God requires a confession of Christian faith before running to His lost children, throwing His arms around them, and welcoming them home.

⁹ Matthew 25:34-40, (NIV)

¹⁰ "Women should remain silent in the churches. They are not allowed to speak, but must be in submission, as the law says. If they want to inquire about something, they should ask their own husbands at home; for it is disgraceful for a woman to speak in the church." 1 Corinthians 14:34-35 (NIV). Writers suggest that this prohibition, while not in the Torah or Old Testament, was a rabbinical practice that had become a firm rule in the temples where Jesus and His Jewish followers worshipped, incorporated into the Talmud circa 200 AD. See, *inter alia,*
http://www.torahforwomen.com/should-women-keep-silent-book.html.

I would be many fathoms out of my depth to try to referee any debate on ancient practices or Jewish scriptures and note only in this superficial way what little I have learned of it.

[11] For a fuller explication of our former church's reasons for interpreting the New Testament to compel gender equality in worship, see, http://www.stamfordchurch.com/#/publications/faith-and-gender

[12] "[T]this business of resentment is infinitely grave. We found that it is fatal. For when harboring such feelings we shut ourselves off from the sunlight of the Spirit. The insanity of alcohol returns and we drink again. And with us, to drink is to die. If we were to live, we had to be free of anger. The grouch and the brainstorm were not for us. They may be the dubious luxury of normal men, but for alcoholics these things are poison." *Alcoholics Anonymous,* p. 66.

[13] 1 Corinthians 13:12 (NLT)

[14] Romans 8:38-39 (NIV)

[15] "Love never fails. But where there are prophecies, they will cease; where there are tongues, they will be stilled; where there is knowledge, it will pass away. For we know in part and we prophesy in part, but when completeness comes, what is in part disappears. When I was a child, I talked like a child, I thought like a child, I reasoned like a child. When I became a man, I put the ways of childhood behind me. For now we see only a reflection as in a mirror; then we shall see face to face. Now I know in part; then I

shall know fully, even as I am fully known." 1 Corinthians 13:8-12, (NIV)

16 Romans 8:28 (NIV)

17 Matthew 5:9 ("Blessed are the peacemakers, for they will be called children of God"), 26:52 ("'Put your sword back in its place,' Jesus said to him, 'for all who draw the sword will die by the sword.'") NIV

18 "Consider it pure joy, my brothers and sisters, whenever you face trials of many kinds, because you know that the testing of your faith produces perseverance. Let perseverance finish its work so that you may be mature and complete, not lacking anything." James 1:2-4, (NIV)

19 *See, e.g.,* "When tempted, no one should say, 'God is tempting me.' For God cannot be tempted by evil, nor does he tempt anyone; but each person is tempted when they are dragged away by their own evil desire and enticed. Then, after desire has conceived, it gives birth to sin; and sin, when it is full-grown, gives birth to death. Don't be deceived, my dear brothers and sisters. Every good and perfect gift is from above, coming down from the Father of the heavenly lights, who does not change like shifting shadows. James 1:13-17 (NIV).

20 John 11:35 (NIV)

21 Matthew 14:26–31 (NIV)

22 The LORD is my shepherd; I shall not want. He maketh me to lie down in green pastures: he leadeth me beside the still waters. He restoreth my soul: he leadeth me in the paths of righteousness for his name's sake. Yea, though I

walk through the valley of the shadow of death, I will fear no evil: for thou art with me; thy rod and thy staff they comfort me. Thou preparest a table before me in the presence of mine enemies: thou anointest my head with oil; my cup runneth over. Surely goodness and mercy shall follow me all the days of my life: and I will dwell in the house of the LORD for ever. Psalm 23 (King James Version).

[23] 2 Corinthians 5:5-9 (NIV) (emphasis added)

[24] My editor thinks someone is interested in why a cancer drug would perforate a nasal septum. For that reader: "In our pts receiving antiangiogenic therapy and chemotherapy, several specific mechanisms could be involved. First, mucositis induced by chemotherapy may weaken nasal mucosa. Nasal irritation due to chemotherapy induced mucositis and/or bevacizumab may induce mucosal breaks and ulcerations. These irritations can be increased by frequent nose blowing and mechanical trauma. Neutropenia frequently associated with chemotherapy enhance the risk of local infection. Bevacizumab decreases normal tissue repair. Bleeding could be seen because of the effect of bevacizumab in wound healing. The inhibition of VEGF can induce a loss of capillaries by apoptosis of endothelial cells, which causes tissue necrosis. Cartilage is not vascularised. The trophicity is maintained by factors from capillaries of mucosa via a terminal vascularisation. In the weakened mucosa, the trophicity of the cartilage might no longer be obtained." *Nasal septum perforation: a side effect of bevacizumab chemotherapy in breast cancer patients,* by Mailliez, Baldini, Van, Servent, Mallet, and Bonneterre, British Journal of Cancer. 2010 Sep 7; 103(6): 772–775.

[25] For the biology nerd who read the last footnote: "It has been theorized that HFSR may occur because keratinocytes in the epidermis synthesize PDGF-α and PDGF-β, which activate PDGFRs located on dermal fibroblasts, capillaries, and eccrine glands [33]. Dermal eccrine glands also express c-KIT and PDGFR, targets of sorafenib. The higher incidence of HFSR when sorafenib is combined with bevacizumab [31] suggests that blockade of both the VEGF and PDGF pathways may hinder vascular repair, thereby triggering HFSR in areas that undergo repeated high-pressure insult, such as palms and soles." *Clinical Presentation and Management of Hand–Foot Skin Reaction Associated with Sorafenib in Combination with Cytotoxic Chemotherapy: Experience in Breast Cancer* by Patricia Gomez, corresponding author, and Mario E. Lacouture,, Oncologist. 2011 Nov; 16(11): 1508–151. Dr. Lacouture, an MSKCC dermatologist, treats my HFSR.

[26] John 11:32-35, (NIV)

[27] Matthew 4:1-11, (NIV)

[28] 1 Peter 5:8, (NIV)

[29] 1 Kings 19:12 (KJV). This is translated as a "gentle whisper" in the NIV.

Made in the USA
Middletown, DE
10 July 2020